麦格希 中英双语阅读文库

影响世界的名人故事

第1辑

【美】布鲁卡 (Milada Broukal) ●主编

杨挺扬●译

麦格希中英双语阅读文库编委会●编

全国百佳图书出版单位

吉林出版集团股份有限公司

图书在版编目（CIP）数据

影响世界的名人故事. 第1辑 / (美) 布鲁卡
(Milada Broukal) 主编 ; 麦格希中英双语阅读文库
编委会编 ; 杨挺扬译. -- 2版. -- 长春 : 吉林出
版集团股份有限公司, 2018.3（2022.1重印）
（麦格希中英双语阅读文库）
ISBN 978-7-5581-4735-7

Ⅰ.①影⋯ Ⅱ.①布⋯ ②麦⋯ ③杨⋯ Ⅲ.①英语—
汉语—对照读物②故事—作品集—世界—现代 Ⅳ.
①H319.4：I

中国版本图书馆CIP数据核字(2018)第055283号

影响世界的名人故事　第1辑

编：麦格希中英双语阅读文库编委会
插　　画：齐　航　李延霞
责任编辑：欧阳鹏
封面设计：冯冯翼
开　　本：660mm×960mm　1/16
字　　数：242千字
印　　张：10.75
版　　次：2018年3月第2版
印　　次：2022年1月第1次印刷

出　　版：吉林出版集团股份有限公司
发　　行：吉林出版集团外语教育有限公司
地　　址：长春市福祉大路5788号龙腾国际大厦B座7层
　　　　　邮编：130011
电　　话：总编办：0431-81629929
　　　　　发行部：0431-81629927　0431-81629921(Fax)
印　　刷：北京一鑫印务有限责任公司

ISBN 978-7-5581-4735-7　　　定价：38.00元
版权所有　　侵权必究　　举报电话：0431-81629929

前言 *PREFACE*

英国思想家培根说过：阅读使人深刻。阅读的真正目的是获取信息，开拓视野和陶冶情操。从语言学习的角度来说，学习语言若没有大量阅读就如隔靴搔痒，因为阅读中的语言是最丰富、最灵活、最具表现力、最符合生活情景的，同时读物中的情节、故事引人入胜，进而能充分调动读者的阅读兴趣，培养读者的文学修养，至此，语言的学习水到渠成。

"麦格希中英双语阅读文库"在世界范围内选材，涉及科普、社会文化、文学名著、传奇故事、成长励志等多个系列，充分满足英语学习者课外阅读之所需，在阅读中学习英语、提高能力。

◎难度适中

本套图书充分照顾读者的英语学习阶段和水平，从读者的阅读兴趣出发，以难易适中的英语语言为立足点，选材精心、编排合理。

◎精品荟萃

本套图书注重经典阅读与实用阅读并举。既包含国内外脍炙人口、耳熟能详的美文，又包含科普、人文、故事、励志类等多学科的精彩文章。

◎功能实用

本套图书充分体现了双语阅读的功能和优势，充分考虑到读者课外阅读的方便，超出核心词表的词汇均出现在使其意义明显的语境之中，并标注释义。

鉴于编者水平有限，凡不周之处，谬误之处，皆欢迎批评教正。

我们真心地希望本套图书承载的文化知识和英语阅读的策略对提高读者的英语著作欣赏水平和英语运用能力有所裨益。

丛书编委会

Contents

William Shakespeare

At the age of one, William Shakespeare was lucky to be alive. After he was born, a *deadly* disease came to England. It was called the *plague*. It killed thousands of people. But William Shakespeare lived.

Shakespeare grew up in Stratford-upon-Avon, England. He went to school

---

威廉·莎士比亚

莎士比亚一岁时幸运地活了下来。他出生不久，英国开始流传一种叫作鼠疫的致命疾病，它夺去了成千上万人的生命，而莎士比亚却活了下来。

莎士比亚在英格兰埃文河畔的斯特拉特福长大。他每周上6天学，每天上9小时课。1582年，在他18岁时娶了农民的女儿、年长他6岁的安

---

deadly *adj.* 致命的   plague *n.* 瘟疫

nine hours a day, six days a week. In 1582, at age 18, he married Anne Hathaway, a farmer's daughter. She was eight years older than he was. Their first child was a daughter. Later they had twins. In 1585, Shakespeare left Stratford-upon-Avon. His wife and children stayed behind. No one knows why he left or what he did between 1585 and 1592.

In 1592, Shakespeare lived in London. He *rented* rooms or lived with friends. He *visited* his wife and family once a year. Shakespeare became an actor, and he also wrote plays. He usually acted in his own plays. Some of his most famous plays were *Romeo and Juliet*, *Hamlet*, and *Macbeth*. He wrote 37 plays in all. They are still popular today.

妮·哈瑟维为妻。他们的第一个孩子是个女孩，后来他们又有了一对双胞胎。1585年莎士比亚只身离开了家乡斯特拉特福。但他的妻儿却留在了那里，没有人知道他为什么出走，也不知道在1585年到1592年期间他都干了些什么。

1592年，莎士比亚定居伦敦。他有时自己租房子，有时和朋友们住在一起。每年他回家一次看自己的妻儿。莎士比亚当了演员，还自己编写剧本。他通常在自己写的剧中饰演角色。他的著名剧作有：《罗密欧与朱丽叶》、《哈姆雷特》和《麦克白》。他一生写了37部剧本，直到今天它们仍颇受人们喜欢。

---

rent *v.* 租   visit *v.* 暂住；访问

Then the plague came again. Many people died. The theaters closed for two years. Shakespeare could not write plays, so he wrote poems. When the theaters opened, Shakespeare wrote plays again. Shakespeare had a theater group. It was the most successful group of that time. Shakespeare earned almost no money from his writing. But he made a lot of money from acting. With this money he bought a large house in Stratford-upon-Avon for his family. He was friendly with the richest people in town. He was a gentleman—a man of high class who didn't have to work.

At age 49, Shakespeare *retired* and went to live in Stratford-upon-Avon. He died at 52. He left his money to his family. He left his *genius* to the world.

其后，鼠疫再次流传，许多人又因此丧命，剧院也关闭了两年。莎士比亚也就不能再写剧本了，于是他开始写诗。当剧院重新开张时，他又拿起笔来写剧本。莎士比亚拥有一个剧团，是当时最成功的剧团。他几乎没有从剧本创作中挣到什么钱，但从演出中挣到了一大笔钱。他用这些钱在斯特拉特福为家人购置了一处大寓所。在城里，他和富人的关系很好。他是一位绅士——可以不工作的上层人物。

莎士比亚49岁退出戏剧界后回到家乡居住，52岁辞世。他把钱财留给了家人，把天才留给了世界。

---

retire *v.* 退休   genius *n.* 天才；天赋

Louis Xiv

Louis became King of France at the age of five when his father died. In the beginning, he was too young to rule, so his mother helped him. Then at age 17, Louis ruled the country alone. He was king for 72 years. France became a *powerful* country with Louis as king. But Louis lived a life of *luxury*, which made people angry.

路易十四

路易5岁时，父王驾崩，他便成了法国国王。继位之初，他过于年幼，没有能力主政，母后不得不辅佐他。到了17岁时，他开始独立执政，在位72年。因有路易国王当政，法国成了强国。但是，路易的奢华生活激起了很大民愤。

powerful *adj.* 强大的   luxury *n.* 奢华

Louis built a huge *palace* at Versailles, near Paris. It took 40 years to finish it. At one time, 36,000 people worked on building the palace. The palace cost so much money that Louis did not let people talk about it. The gardens of the palace had 1,400 *fountains*. The fountains used a lot of water so they worked for only three hours at a time.

The fountains used water, but Louis did not! He hated to wash. He took only three baths in his life. He washed only one part of his body—the tip of the nose. Everyone in the palace had to do what the king did, so people washed only their noses!

Louis XIV had other unusual rules. He liked to keep the windows open at the palace. He wanted dozens of people around him when he got dressed. Also, only the king and queen could sit on chairs

---

在巴黎附近的凡尔赛，路易建造了宏伟的皇宫，历时四十余年才完工，期间曾经一次就投入劳力三万六千多人。耗费如此巨大，怨声载道，以至于路易不许老百姓议论此事。皇宫的花园有1400座喷泉。由于喷泉耗用大量的水，因此，这些喷泉一次只能喷洒3个小时。

喷泉如此大量用水，而路易则相反！他厌恶洗澡，他一辈子只洗过3次澡，平时他只洗身体的一小部分——鼻子尖而已。皇宫里所有的人不得不仿效他，也只能洗他们的鼻子尖。

路易十四还有另一些不寻常的规矩。他喜欢皇宫里的窗户一直打开着，他穿衣时要数十人围着他，而且只有他和王后才能坐有扶手的椅子，其他人只能坐没有扶手的椅子。

---

palace *n.* 宫殿

fountain *n.* 喷泉

with arms. Everybody else had to sit on chairs with no arms.

Louis had problems sleeping. People say that he had 413 beds. He went from one bed to another until he fell asleep. But he had a good *appetite*. A normal dinner for Louis was four bowls of soup, two whole chickens, ham, lamb, a salad, cakes, fruit, and hard-boiled eggs. He also drank a lot of *champagne* because his doctor told him to. He lived to be 77 years old. When he died, doctors said his stomach was two times the size of a normal stomach.

Louis XIV was not always popular, but he was an important king in the history of France. He was so important that he was called "the Sun King."

路易睡觉有个怪癖，据说他有413张床，他会从一张床换到另一张床，直到睡着为止。然而，他胃口极好，平常一顿饭，他要喝4碗汤，吃两只整鸡、火腿、羔羊肉、色拉、糕点、水果和煮得透熟的鸡蛋。他还要喝许多香槟酒，这是遵从医生的吩咐。他活到77岁。他死后，医生说他的胃是正常人的两倍大。

路易十四并不总是家喻户晓的，但他在法国历史上是个非常重要的国王，以致他被称为"太阳王"。

---

appetite *n.* 食欲   champagne *n.* 香槟酒

3

Florence **N**ightingale

Florence Nightingale was English, but she was born in Italy. Her parents named her Florence, after the city. Her family was rich, so Florence *grew up* with everything she wanted. When she became a young woman, her parents wanted her to get married. But Florence did not want to

佛罗伦萨·南丁格尔

佛罗伦萨·南丁格尔是位英国人，但出生在意大利。她父母用佛罗伦萨市的市名给她起的名字。她家很富有，所以，南丁格尔在成长过程中想要什么都有求必应。她长成大姑娘时，父母想让她结婚，

---

grow up *成长*

MCGRAW-HILL

get married. She wanted to be a nurse. Her parents were angry. In those days, hospitals were dirty places. Respectable women did not work in hospitals. But Florence did not listen to her parents. She studied to be a nurse. Soon, she *supervised* a hospital for women in London. She was a great success.

In 1854, there was a war. Many British soldiers were in a hospital in Turkey. The hospital needed help. Florence Nightingale *volunteered* to go to Turkey. She brought 38 nurses to help her. When she got there, 42 percent of the soldiers in the hospital were dying. The hospital was very dirty. There was not enough food or clothing for the sick. Nightingale and her nurses started to clean and put the hospital in order. In just one month only 2 percent of the soldiers were dying! Nightingale worked 20 hours a day. Every night she

---

而南丁格尔不想结婚，她想当护士，为此父母非常生气。那时候，医院很脏，有身份的女人不会去医院工作。但南丁格尔不听从父母的，她学习医护，打算当一名护士。很快，她负责管理伦敦一家为妇女开设的医院，并获得了巨大成功。

1854年爆发了一场战争。许多英国伤兵住进了土耳其的一家医院，因此这家医院需要帮助。南丁格尔带了38名护士志愿奔赴土耳其。赶到那里时，医院伤兵的死亡率是42%。医院很脏，伤病员们没有足够的食品和衣服。南丁格尔和护士们开始打扫卫生，把医院整理得井井有条。仅仅一个月，士兵的死亡率就降到2%。南丁格尔每天工作20个小时。每天夜晚

---

supervise *v.* 监督；管理

volunteer *v.* 志愿

walked around the hospital with her lamp. She comforted the sick soldiers. The soldiers loved her. They called her the "Lady with the Lamp." Her story was in the newspapers in England, and she became famous. Even Queen Victoria, the *queen* of England, wanted to meet her.

After two years, Nightingale went back to England. She was very sick, but she still worked. She started a school for nurses. The school continues to this day. Nightingale never married. But she did not live alone. She had 60 cats. When she was 43, Nightingale became sick. She was in bed for the rest of her life. She continued to work to help others. She died at age 90. We remember Florence Nightingale because she helped make nursing the important *profession* that it is today.

她都要提着灯巡查病房，安慰、扶助伤病员。战士们都爱戴她，他们称她为"擎灯女士"。英国各报刊载了她的事迹，她成了名人，甚至英国的维多利亚女王也要会见她。

两年后，南丁格尔返回英国。她得了重病，但是她仍然坚持工作。她开办了一所护士学校，这所学校一直办到今天。南丁格尔终身未嫁，但她生活得并不孤独。她养了60只猫。43岁时，她病倒了，在床上度过了余生。但是她继续从事帮助他人的工作。她90岁时谢世。我们怀念佛罗伦萨·南丁格尔，因为她的努力，使护理工作能像今天这样成为一种重要的职业。

queen *n.* 女王　　　　　　　　　　　　profession *n.* 职业

Emily Dickinson

Emily Dickinson was a very famous American poet. She wrote about 2,000 *poems*, but only four were *published* in her lifetime. No one wanted to publish her work because it was different from what other poets wrote. After Dickinson died, her poems were finally published. Then she became famous.

艾米丽·迪金森

艾米丽·迪金森是一位非常著名的美国诗人。她一生写了大约两千首诗，但她在世时只有四首诗被发表了。因为她写诗的风格与当时的诗风很不相同，所以没有人想发表她的作品。去世后，她的诗作终于得以发表，她也因此而成名。

poem *n.* 诗   publish *v.* 发表

Some things about Emily Dickinson's life are strange and *mysterious*. She was born in 1830 in Amherst, Massachusetts, to a rich and well-known family. She had a brother and a sister. Emily was shy and quiet, but she had friends. She went to parties like other young girls her age and met young men. But she did not fall in love with any of them and never married.

After a while, Emily Dickinson did not want to see her friends. She stayed home. She read, worked in the garden, and wrote *poetry*. Dickinson wrote her poems everywhere. She wrote them on bits of newspaper or anything that was near. Later, she wrote them out carefully. When she was 28, something happened. Dickinson was very upset. No one knows why. Some people say she loved a married man. Others say she was unhappy because nobody wanted

---

　　艾米丽·迪金森生活中的一些事有些古怪和神秘。她1830年生于美国马萨诸塞州阿默斯特镇的一个声名显赫的富有家庭，有一个哥哥和一个姐姐。虽然艾米丽是个腼腆、文静的女孩，但她有许多朋友。像同龄女孩一样，她参加聚会，会见男孩子。但她从没有与他们中的任何一个谈过恋爱，并终身未嫁。

　　一段时间以后，艾米丽·迪金森不想再去会见朋友了。她在家中的花园里读书、干活和写诗。她随时随地写诗，常常把诗写在报纸的边角处或手边的任何东西上，尔后再认真地把它们整理出来。28岁时，发生的一些事使她非常苦恼。没有人知道这是为什么，有人说她爱上了一个有妇之夫，也有人说她不高兴是因为没有人愿意发表她的诗集。不管怎样，她还

---

mysterious *adj.* 神秘的　　　　　　　　　　　　poetry *n.* 诗

to publish her poetry. She continued to write anyway.

As she got older, Dickinson wanted to be alone more often. When someone came to the house, she ran upstairs to *hide*. For the last 16 years of her life, she never left her home. The *curtains* were always closed. She dressed only in white. One day Dickinson became ill, but she did not let the doctor in her room. He could only see her from the doorway.

Dickinson died at the age of 55. Her sister found her poems, and they were finally published. Sadly, Emily Dickinson did not live to enjoy her great success.

是继续写诗。

随着年龄的增长，她变得愈来愈孤独。有人去她的住处，她就到楼上躲起来。在她生命的最后16年里，她从未离开过家，家里的窗帘总是紧闭着。她只穿白色衣服。一天，她病了，却不让医生进她的房间，医生只能从门外的过道处给她看病。

艾米丽·迪金森55岁谢世。姐姐发现了她的诗作，这些诗歌终于被发表了。令人感到惋惜的是，她没能在活着的时候享受到成功的喜悦。

---

hide *v.* 隐藏　　　　　　　　　　　curtain *n.* 窗帘

5

Peter Ilich Tchaikovsky

Peter Ilich Tchaikovsky was born in 1840 in Russia. His family was rich and sent him to special schools. Tchaikovsky went to a university and studied law. But at the age of 23, he decided to give his life to music. He studied music in Saint Petersburg. When he was 26, he wrote his first *symphony*.

Tchaikovsky became a famous and successful *composer*. But he did not live a happy or exciting life. He was very shy and lived

---

彼得·伊利奇·柴可夫斯基

得·伊利奇·柴可夫斯基1840年出生于俄国。他家境富裕，并被送到特殊的学校读书。在大学他攻读法律。然而在23岁时，他决定毕生致力于音乐，并在圣彼得堡学习音乐。26岁时谱写了他的第一部交响曲。

柴可夫斯基在这方面获得了成功，成了一位著名的作曲家。但他的生活不幸福，同时也缺乏激情。他很内向，不善与人交往，因此生活孤独，

---

symphony *n.* 交响乐   composer *n.* 作曲家

alone. Every day he stayed home and wrote music. He was often unhappy. He was afraid of many things. He was afraid to die. He was also afraid his head would fall off his *shoulders*. This was a problem when he *conducted* music. So he sometimes held his head with his left hand and conducted with his right hand.

In 1876, Tchaikovsky received a letter from a mysterious rich widow. Her name was Madame von Meck. She said she loved his

每天就待在家里作曲。他经常不开心，很多事令他害怕。他怕死，还担心脑袋会从肩上掉下来。这成了他指挥乐队时的难题。因此，有时候他用左手托着脑袋，用右手指挥。

　　1876年，柴可夫斯基收到一封来自一位神秘而富有的寡妇的信，她

shoulder *n.* 肩　　　　　　　　　　　　　　conduct *v.* 指挥

music and offered to send him money every year. There was one condition. They must never meet. Tchaikovsky agreed. They wrote to each other for 14 years. Then Madame von Meck suddenly stopped writing. Tchaikovsky was very hurt. When he died three years later, he said her name.

Tchaikovsky died after he drank *contaminated* water. He was 53. Some people say he drank it by accident. Others say he drank the water to kill himself. Today we remember Tchaikovsky for his wonderful symphonies and *ballets*. To this day, *Swan Lake*, *The Sleeping Beauty*, and *The Nutcracker* are three of the world's most popular ballets.

叫梅克夫人，并说她喜欢他的音乐，愿意每年寄钱给他。但有一个条件，他们绝不能见面。柴可夫斯基答应了。他们通信持续了14年，后来梅克夫人突然中断了书信。柴可夫斯基非常伤心，3年后他去世时还念念不忘她的名字。

柴可夫斯基饮用了有毒的水后身亡，享年53岁。有人说他是误饮，有人说他是有意自杀。今天，我们怀念柴可夫斯基，难忘他美妙的交响曲和芭蕾舞曲。直到今天，《天鹅湖》、《睡美人》和《胡桃夹子》仍然是世界上最受欢迎的三部芭蕾舞曲。

---

contaminated *adj.* 受污染的   ballet *n.* 芭蕾舞乐曲

Marie Curie

Marie Curie was a great *scientist*. She was born Marja Sklodowska in Warsaw, Poland, in 1867. Both of her parents were teachers. When Marie was only 10 years old, her mother died.

Marie was a very good student. She loved science, math, and *languages*. She and her sister Bronya

88
Ra
Radium
226.0254

玛丽·居里

玛丽·居里是一位伟大的科学家。1867年生于波兰华沙，原名为玛丽亚·斯克洛多夫斯卡。她的父母都是教师。玛丽10岁时母亲去世了。

玛丽是位好学生。她喜欢科学、数学和语言，和姐姐布罗安亚一样

---

scientist *n.* 科学家   language *n.* 语言

wanted to go to college. But in those days, only men could go to college in Poland. The girls had to go to France to study. There was not enough money for both sisters to go. So Marie worked as a teacher in Poland. She sent money to Bronya to pay for medical school in Paris. After Bronya became a doctor, she helped Marie.

When she was 24, Marie became a *science* student at the Sorbonne, a university in Paris. Even with her sister's help, she did not have much money. She lived in a small room near the college. It had no lights, no water, and no heat. Sometimes Marie only had bread and tea to eat.

Marie studied hard and graduated in 1894. A year later, she married Pierre Curie. He was also a scientist. They worked together for many years. Their most important discovery was *radium*. Today,

想上大学，但在那个时候，波兰只允许男子读大学，而女子只能去法国求学。由于姐妹俩没有足够的钱一起去法国读书，所以玛丽在波兰做教师，寄钱给姐姐支付巴黎医学院的学费。后来布罗安亚当了医生，她再资助玛丽读书。

玛丽24岁时，成了索邦神学院(巴黎大学的前身)的理科学生。即便有姐姐的资助，玛丽也没有多少钱。她住在大学附近的一间小屋里。屋里没有灯，没有水，没有暖气。玛丽时常靠面包和茶来充饥。

玛丽刻苦学习，于1894年毕业。一年后，她和皮埃尔·居里结婚。皮埃尔也是一位科学家，他们一起工作了许多年。他们的最大成就是发现

science *n.* 理科   radium *n.* 镭

doctors use the rays from radium to treat cancer. The Curies won a Nobel Prize for their discovery. This is the highest award for a scientist. Marie Curie was the first woman to receive this *award*.

When Marie Curie was 39, Pierre died in a road accident. But she continued their work. Curie became the first woman *professor* in France. In 1911, she won a second Nobel Prize. But years of working with radium ruined her health. She died of cancer in 1934. Her daughter Irene continued Curie's work. She also received a Nobel Prize. Sadly, Irene also got cancer and died young. Both women gave their lives for their work.

了镭。今天，医生用镭射线治疗癌症。居里夫妇因此而获得诺贝尔奖，这是科学家的最高奖项。玛丽·居里是获得这一奖项的第一名女性。

玛丽·居里39岁时，皮埃尔死于一起交通事故。但居里夫人仍然继续他们共同的研究工作，并成为法国第一位女教授。1911年，她第二次荣获诺贝尔奖。由于长期和镭打交道，她的健康严重受损，1934年居里夫人因癌症去世。她的女儿伊雷娜继续从事居里夫人的工作，同样也获得了诺贝尔奖。但令人悲痛的是，她也得了癌症，英年早逝。两位杰出的女性为工作献出了她们宝贵的生命。

---

award *n.* 奖品   professor *n.* 教授

Madam
C. J. Walker

Madam C. J. Walker was the first African American woman in the United States to make a million dollars. She was born Sarah Breedlove in 1867 on a farm in Delta, Louisiana. Her family was very poor, and her life was very hard. They lived in a small house with a dirt floor and no windows. Sarah did not go to school. Every day she worked from morning to night in the *cotton* fields.

When Sarah was seven, her parents died. She went to Mississippi to live with her married sister. Her sister's husband was very *mean*

C. J. 华尔克夫人

C. J. 华尔克夫人是美国第一位身价超过百万的非洲裔美国人。她于1867年出生在路易斯安那州德尔塔的一个农场，原名叫萨拉·布里德勒乌。她家境贫寒，生活艰辛，全家住的小屋是泥土地面，没有窗户。萨拉上不起学，每天从早到晚都在棉花地里干活。

萨拉7岁时父母双亡，已婚的姐姐住在密西西比州，她就住在姐姐

---

cotton *n.* 棉花　　　　　　　　　　　　　mean *adj.* 卑鄙的；低劣的

to her. Sarah wanted to get away, so she got married when she was 14. A few years later, she had a baby girl named Lelia. When Sarah was only 20, her husband died. She moved to St. Louis, Missouri. For the next 18 years, she worked washing clothes for $1.50 a day. When she was 38, Sarah was

worried because her hair was falling out. She tried different things on her hair, but nothing worked. One night she had a dream about what to *mix up* and use for her hair. It worked! Sarah gave it to her friends. It worked for them, too. She went from door to door to sell her new

---

家。姐夫对她很不好，她想离开那个家。因此，14岁时她就结婚了。几年后生了个女儿，起名叫莱丽娅。萨拉年仅20岁时，她的丈夫就去世了。萨拉移居到密苏里州的圣路易斯。接下来的18个年头里，她一直以洗衣为生，每天挣1.5美元。38岁时，她感到很苦恼，因为头发一直在掉。她试了很多办法，但全都无济于事。一天夜里，她梦见把一些东西调和起来，抹在头发上，效果很好。醒来后照着去做，果然奏效！萨拉把这些调和物赠给朋友使用，效果也很好。她挨家挨户地兜售她的新护发精，随后她又生产了其他新的护发品。不久，她有了自己的产业。

---

mix up 混合

hair product. Then she made other hair care products. Soon she had her own business.

Sarah Breedlove married Charles Joseph Walker and opened several beauty shops under the name of Madam C. J. Walker. In 1910, she built a factory to make hair care products and face creams. By 1917, her company was the most successful African American-owned business in the United States. She started her business with only $1.50, but now she was rich. She had a *mansion* in New York. Madam Walker also gave a lot of money to charity. She wanted to help *African Americans*, especially women. But she did not enjoy her good life for very long. Madam Walker died at the age of 52. She left two-thirds of her fortune to charity. Her will said that the head of the C. J. Walker Company must always be a woman.

萨拉·布里德勒乌和查尔斯·约瑟夫·华尔克结了婚，并以C. J. 华尔克夫人的名字开了几家美容店。1910年，她建了一家工厂生产护发品和面霜。到1917年，她的公司成了全美非洲裔美国人经营的最为成功的公司。她仅以1.5美元起家，而到那时她已很富有了。她在纽约有一座大厦，还捐了许多钱给慈善团体。她愿意帮助非裔美国人，特别是妇女。不过她并没有享受多久好生活，52岁就去世了。她把自己2/3的财产捐赠给了慈善事业。她在遗嘱中提出，C. J. 华尔克公司的最高领导必须永远是一位女性。

---

mansion *n.* 大厦   African American 非裔美国人

8

Albert Einstein

Albert Einstein is one of the greatest scientists who ever lived. But he couldn't find his way home when he went for a walk. He dressed in *wrinkled* clothes and an old coat. He often forgot things. Once he used a $1,500 check to mark a page in a book. Then he lost the book! Einstein had other things to think about. Science was more important to him than the ordinary things in life.

Albert Einstein was born in 1879 in Ulm, Germany. When he was a child, he learned things very slowly. Albert didn't speak until he was three years old. His parents worried about him. The *principal*

阿尔伯特·爱因斯坦

阿尔伯特·爱因斯坦是人类史上最伟大的科学家之一。可是，他外出散步时竟会找不到回家的路。他穿着皱巴巴的衣服，常穿一件旧外套，还经常忘事。一次，他用一张1500美元的支票夹在书里做书签。后来，他却弄丢了那本书。爱因斯坦有其他的事情要考虑。对他来说，科学比那些生活琐事更为重要。

阿尔伯特·爱因斯坦1879年出生在德国的乌尔姆镇。儿时，他学东西很慢，3岁才会说话。父母很为他担心。校长曾对他父亲说："你儿子

---

wrinkled *adj.* 有皱纹的　　　　　　　　　　　principal *n.* 校长

of his school told his father, "Your son will never make a success of anything." His grades in school were bad. The only thing he liked to do was to play the violin.

When he was 12, Albert began reading math and science books. He was *excited* about the things he learned. At age 17, he started college in Switzerland. Einstein wanted to be a teacher. He *graduated* in 1900, but he could not find a job. A friend helped him get a job in a government office.

While he was in school, Einstein became more and more interested in math and physics. He wanted to find the answers to

---

做什么事都不会成功。"他的学习成绩很差。他唯一的爱好就是拉小提琴。

12岁时，阿尔伯特开始阅读数学和科学书籍，他对学到的知识很兴奋。17岁时他到瑞士读大学，爱因斯坦的理想是当一名教师，1900年毕业后却找不到一份工作。一位朋友帮他在政府部门谋到一份差事。

在校时，爱因斯坦对数学和物理愈来愈感兴趣。他想找到有关宇宙问

---

excited *adj.* 兴奋的   graduate *v.* 毕业

questions about the universe. In 1905, Einstein published his ideas. At first, other scientists laughed at them. But Einstein's *theory* of *relativity* changed the world. Scientists looked at the universe in a new way. Because of Einstein, we have such things as computers, television, and space travel today.

Einstein quickly became famous. He traveled around the world and talked about his ideas. In 1922, he received the Nobel Prize for physics. In 1933, Adolf Hitler came to power in Germany. Life became difficult for Jews like Einstein. So Einstein moved to America. He lived and taught in Princeton, New Jersey, for 22 years until he died in 1955. He once said, " The important thing is not to stop questioning." Albert Einstein never did.

题的答案。1905年发表了他的论文。起初，遭到了其他科学家的讥讽。但是，爱因斯坦的相对论改变了世界科学。科学家们用一种新方法观察宇宙。由于爱因斯坦的理论，我们才有了计算机和电视，才能到太空旅行。

爱因斯坦很快声名鹊起。他周游世界，宣讲他的理论。1922年，他荣获诺贝尔物理奖。1933年，当时希特勒当政，像爱因斯坦一样的犹太人的生活变得很艰难。因此，爱因斯坦移居到美国。他居住并执教于新泽西州的普林斯顿(大学)达22年之久，直到1955年去世。他曾说："重要的是，不要停止提出问题。"阿尔伯特·爱因斯坦从未停止过发问和探索。

---

theory *n.* 理论　　　　　　　　　　　　　　relativity *n.* 相对

9

Pablo Picasso

Pablo Picasso drew pictures before he could talk. As a child, he sat happily with his paper and pencils and drew for hours. His father was a painter. He was very happy that his son liked to draw, but he did not know that one day Pablo would be one of the greatest *artists* of the twentieth century.

Pablo Picasso was born in 1881 in Malaga, Spain. He was a very bad student, and he *hated* school. Instead of studying, he drew pictures. When he was only eight years old, he finished his first oil painting. It had beautiful colors. Picasso never sold this painting.

巴勃罗·毕加索

巴勃罗·毕加索还不会说话时就会画画。他还是个孩子的时候，就能高高兴兴地坐在那里用纸和铅笔绘画，一画就是几个小时。毕加索的父亲是个画家，儿子喜欢绘画，他非常高兴。不过，他并不知道将来有一天毕加索会成为20世纪最伟大的画家之一。

1881年毕加索出生在西班牙的马拉加。他不是个好学生，他讨厌学校，不喜欢学习，只爱画画。年仅8岁，他就完成了他的第一幅油画，色彩非常绚丽。毕加索从未出售过这幅画。

---

artist *n.* 艺术家；美术家　　　　　　　　　　　　hate *v.* 憎恨；厌恶

When Pablo was 14, his family moved to Barcelona. He wanted to go to the School of Fine Arts. To get into the school, a student had to finish a painting in one month. Picasso finished his painting in one day.

When he was 18, Picasso went to live in Paris. He was very poor at first. He lived in a small room and worked with only the light of a candle. Sometimes he did not even have money for a candle. But Pablo Picasso had a strong *personality*. He believed in himself. He created one piece of art after another. He met important people, and they began to buy his work. *Eventually* Picasso became rich and famous.

　　巴勃罗·毕加索14岁时，他们全家移居巴塞罗那。他想进美术学校学习。要想入学的学生，必须在一个月之内完成一幅画，而毕加索一天就完成了。

　　18岁时，毕加索移居巴黎。起初，他很穷，住在一间小屋里，只能借助烛光画画，有时甚至连买蜡烛的钱都没有。但毕加索个性坚强，也非常自信，创作出一件又一件作品。他遇到了大人物，这些人开始购买他的作品。毕加索终于成了富人并出了名。

---

personality *n.* 个性　　　　　　　　　　eventually *adv.* 最后，终于

Picasso was strange in many ways. For example, for a long time, he did not want a telephone. Then one day his son almost died because he could not call for help. Picasso was also strange because he did not throw anything away, not even an empty cigarette package. He liked to be alone, so he locked his *studio*. No one could get in. Picasso loved animals. He had a monkey, a goat, *snakes*, and many dogs. He was married twice, and he was not very close to his family and friends. His work was more important to him than people were.

Picasso lived a long and full life. He never stopped working. He painted 200 pictures the year he was 90. He was still working on the day he died at the age of 91. Picasso left the world the genius of his art.

毕加索在许多方面都很古怪。比如，他会很长时间不用电话。有一天，他儿子因无法打电话求助而差点死掉。毕加索还有一个怪异之处，他从不扔掉任何东西，甚至连一个空烟盒也不丢掉。他喜欢独处，锁上他的画室，谁也进不去。毕加索喜欢动物，他养了一只猴子，一只山羊，还有一些蛇和许多狗。他结过两次婚。毕加索不太恋家，和朋友的关系也不密切。对他来说，工作比家人和朋友更为重要。

毕加索高寿且生活充实。他从没有停止过工作。90岁那一年他就画了200幅画。在91岁去世的那一天，他仍然在工作。毕加索给世界留下了他天才的艺术。

---

studio *n.* 工作室　　　　　　　　　　　　　　　snake *n.* 蛇

10

Jean Paul Getty

Jean Paul Getty was born in 1892 in Minneapolis, Minnesota. He became a *millionaire* when he was only 24. His father was *wealthy*, but he did not help his son. Getty made his millions alone. Like his father, he made his money from oil. He owned Getty Oil and over 100 other companies. One magazine called Getty "the richest man in the world."

杰恩·保罗·格蒂

1892年杰恩·保罗·格蒂生于美国明尼苏达州的明尼阿波利斯市。24岁时他就成了百万富翁。他父亲很富有，但这和他毫无关系，格蒂独自创造了百万财富。像父亲一样，他靠石油赚钱。除了格蒂石油公司，他还拥有另外一百多家公司。一家杂志称格蒂是"世界上最大的富豪"。

millionaire *n.* 百万富翁   wealthy *adj.* 富有的

But money did not buy happiness for Getty. He married five times and *divorced* five times. He had five children but spent little time with them. None of Getty's children had very happy lives.

Getty cared a lot about money. He loved to make money and loved to save it. He was a very *stingy* man. Every evening, he wrote down every cent he spent that day. He lived in England in a house with 72 bedrooms. He put pay telephones in his guests' bedrooms so he could save money on phone bills.

In 1973, kidnappers took his grandson. They asked for money to

---

然而，对格蒂来说，金钱买不来幸福。他结过5次婚，又离过5次婚，有5个子女，却很少有时间陪孩子们；他的子女也没有一个生活得幸福。

格蒂非常看重金钱，他既喜欢挣钱，也喜欢存钱。他非常吝啬，甚至每晚他都记录下当天花掉的每一分钱。他在英国的住所有72间卧室，但客房里却全装的是投币电话，为的是节省话费。

1973年，劫匪绑架了格蒂的孙子，扬言要用钱来赎孩子。格蒂的儿

---

divorce *v.* 离婚   stingy *adj.* 吝啬的

release the boy. Getty's son asked his father for money to save his child. Getty refused. So the *kidnappers* cut off the boy's ear. Finally, Getty lent the money to his son, but at 4 percent interest.

Getty had another side. He loved to collect art. He started a museum at his home in Malibu, California. He bought many important and beautiful pieces of art for the museum. When Getty died in 1976, the *value* of the art in the museum was $1 billion. He left all his money to the museum. After his death, the museum grew in size. Today it is one of the most important museums in the United States. Getty made his money from oil. But he gave his money to the art world because he wanted people to learn about and love art.

子请求他拿钱去营救孙子，被格蒂一口拒绝。因此，劫匪割掉了孩子的一只耳朵。最后，格蒂虽把钱借给了儿子，却要收取4％的利息。

格蒂也有不吝啬的一面，他喜欢收藏艺术品。他在美国加利福尼亚州马利布的家里创办了一座博物馆，并为博物馆购置了许多珍贵、精美的艺术品。1976年他去世时，该博物馆的艺术品价值已达10亿美元。格蒂把他所有的钱都捐给了博物馆。他去世以后，该博物馆的规模成倍扩大，如今已成了美国最重要的博物馆之一。格蒂通过石油赚钱，但他把钱奉献给了艺术世界，因为他希望人们都能了解和热爱艺术。

---

kidnapper *n.* 绑匪　　　　　　　　　　　　　　　value *n.* 价值

Oseola McCarty

In 1995, Oseola McCarty gave a gift of $150,000 to the University of Southern Mississippi. She wanted to help poor students. It was a very *generous* thing to do. But her friends and neighbors were surprised. McCarty was a good woman. She went to *church*. She was always friendly and helpful. But

Oseola McCarty

奥塞拉·麦卡蒂

1995年，奥塞拉·麦卡蒂捐赠15万美元给南密西西比大学，来帮助穷苦学生。这一慷慨之举，令她的朋友和邻居惊讶不已。麦卡蒂非常善良。她常去教堂，一贯对人友好，并乐于助人。然而镇上人人都知道她并不富有，实际上她很穷。

---

generous *adj.* 慷慨的   church *n.* 教堂

everyone in her town knew that McCarty was not rich. In fact, she was poor.

How did a poor 86-year-old woman have so much money? Oseola McCarty was born in 1908 in Hattiesburg, Mississippi. She had to leave school when she was eight years old to help her family. She took a job washing clothes. She earned only a few dollars a day. Oseola washed the clothes by hand. Then she *hung* the clothes to dry. She did this for nearly 80 years. In the 1960s, she bought an automatic washer and dryer. But she gave them away. She did not think they got the clothes clean enough! At that time, many people started to buy their own washers and dryers. McCarty did not have much work, so she started to *iron* clothes instead.

一个86岁的穷老太太怎么会有如此多的钱呢？麦卡蒂1908年出生在密西西比州的哈蒂斯堡。8岁时，她不得不辍学去挣钱补贴家用。她找到一份洗衣工作，一天只能挣几美元。她用手洗衣服，然后再挂起来晾干。这项工作她做了将近八十年。20世纪60年代，麦卡蒂购置了自动洗衣机和烘干机，但没多久就不用了，她认为用洗衣机洗不干净。这时候许多人已经开始用洗衣机和烘干机，她没有什么工作好做了。因此，她改做熨烫衣服。

---

hang *v.* 悬挂

iron *v.* 熨烫

McCarty never married or had children. Her life was very simple. She went to work and to church. She read her *Bible*. She had a black-and-white television. But she did not watch it very much. It had only one *channel*.

McCarty saved money all her life and eventually had about $250,000. When she was 86, a lawyer helped her make a will. She left money to the church, her relatives, and the university. McCarty just wanted to help others. She did not think she was a special person. But then people found out about her gift to the university. She received many honors. She even flew in an airplane for the first time!

Oseola McCarty died in 1999. She was a shy and humble woman who became famous.

　　麦卡蒂没有结过婚，无儿无女。她生活得非常简朴。她去工作，上教堂，读圣经。她有一台黑白电视机，但不常看，而且电视机只有一个频道。

　　麦卡蒂一辈子都在攒钱，最后总共攒了约二十五万美元。86岁时，律师帮她立下遗嘱。她把钱留给教堂、亲戚和一所大学。麦卡蒂只是想帮助别人，她不认为自己是个与众不同的人。人们知道了她给大学的捐赠，于是她获得了许多荣誉，她甚至平生第一次坐上了飞机。

　　麦卡蒂1999年去世。这位腼腆、谦逊的妇女成了名人。

Bible *n.* 圣经　　　　　　　　　　　　　　　　　channel *n.* 频道

Babe Didrikson Zaharisa

Babe Didrikson Zaharias was one of the greatest American *athletes* of modern times. She was born Mildred Didrikson in 1911 in Port Arthur, Texas. As a child, she played baseball, basketball, and *tennis*. She also enjoyed running and other sports. Mildred was great at all

Babe
Didrickson
Zaharisa

巴比·迪德里克松·扎哈里爱斯

巴比·迪德里克松·扎哈里爱斯是美国当代最伟大的运动员之一。1911年她出生在得克萨斯州的阿瑟港，原名叫米尔德里德·迪德里克松。还是孩子的时候她就爱打棒球、篮球和网球，她还喜欢跑步和其他运动。米尔德里德在这些方面都很优秀。一天，她在棒球运动中击中5个本垒打，人们因此都叫她"巴比"，那是借用了著名棒球运动员巴比·鲁斯的名字。

---

athlete *n.* 运动员　　　　　　　　　　　　tennis *n.* 网球

of them. One day she hit five home runs in a baseball game. Then everyone called her "Babe" after the famous baseball player Babe Ruth.

Zaharias had many interests. She was very *talented*. She played musical instruments. She sewed clothes very well, and she won first prize at a state fair. She became an excellent ballroom dancer and a great chef. But she liked sports best.

In 1932, Zaharias tried out for the *Olympic games*. She won four events in three hours. Her performance was the greatest in the history of athletics. During the games, she won two gold medals and one silver medal.

Everyone said that Zaharias was a great athlete. But they also

---

扎哈里爱斯兴趣广泛，且天赋很高。她能弹奏乐器，服装做得也很好，曾在州交易会上获一等奖。她还是一名优秀的交际舞舞蹈家和厨师。不过，她还是最喜欢体育。

1932年，她参加了奥林匹克运动会，在3小时之内获得了4个奖项。她是运动史上最为伟大的运动员，这次运动会上她荣获两枚金牌和一枚银牌。

大家都说扎哈里爱斯是一位伟大的运动员。但也有人对此不屑一顾，

---

talented *adj.* 有才能的；天资高的   Olympic games 奥林匹克运动会

said bad things about her because she was a woman. In those days, many women did not work. People believed that women should stay at home. Zaharias was lonely and hurt sometimes. Then she married professional wrestler George Zaharias. He left his job to be Zahariass manager. People said things about that, too!

Zaharias decided to *concentrate* on golf. She practiced 16 hours a day. Sometimes her hands were bloody from practicing. She became a champion. She won 82 tournaments.

Sadly, Babe Didrikson Zaharias died at a young age. She was 45. She was the only female sports hero of her time. She was an important role model for *female* athletes in the United States.

因为她是名妇女。在那个时候，人们认为妇女不应工作，应待在家里。扎哈里爱斯有时感到孤独和伤心。后来，她和职业摔跤运动员乔治哈里爱斯结了婚。她的丈夫放弃了工作，当了她的经纪人，人们对此也说三道四。

扎哈里爱斯决定集中精力打高尔夫球。她每天训练长达16个小时，有时练得双手出血。她当上了冠军，赢得了82场锦标赛的胜利。

令人悲痛的是，巴比·迪德里克松·扎哈里爱斯英年早逝，享年仅45岁。她是那个时代唯一的体育界女英雄，为美国女运动员树立了光辉的榜样。

---

concentrate *v.* 集中精力   female *adj.* 女性的

13

Minoru Yamasaki

Minoru Yamasaki was a *well-known* American architect. He was born in 1912 in Seattle, Washington. His parents came from Japan. Minoru went to college to study *architecture*. Every summer he worked in a fish factory to help pay for college. Often he worked from four o'clock in the morning until midnight. He slept in a room with 100 other men. Later in life, Yamasaki remembered these times and was always good to his workers.

Yamasaki sometimes dreamed about his work. Once he woke up at three o'clock in the morning. He remembered a building that was in his dream. He got up and started to draw. Yamasaki used a

山崎实

山崎实是一位著名的美国建筑师。1912年，他出生在华盛顿州的西雅图市，他的祖籍是日本。山崎实上大学时主修建筑。每年暑假，他都在一家鱼肉加工厂打工攒学费，经常从凌晨4点一直忙到午夜。他睡的那间屋子里除他之外，还有另外100号人。后来，山崎一直未曾忘却这段艰苦岁月，将心比心，对自己的员工也就非常好。

山崎实有时做梦都梦到工作。一次，凌晨3点他就醒了，回忆起梦中的一幢建筑，就马上起床开始画图。山崎对建筑物采用了新式设计，这些

well-known *adj.* 著名的　　　　　　　architecture *n.* 建筑学

new design for the buildings. These buildings are now the Century Plaza Hotel and Tower in Los Angeles, California.

Minoru Yamasaki

Yamasaki was different from other architects. His buildings give people a feeling of *peace* and happiness. Many of his designs have pools of water, flowers, and windows on the *roof* to let in light. He always designed buildings to please people. He wanted to give them a place away from the busy ways of modern life.

Yamasaki worked for several companies. But his success began when he started his own company. In 1956, he won the Architect's

---

建筑物包括现在位于加利福尼亚州的洛杉矶世纪广场的酒店和塔楼。

山崎实和其他建筑师不同，他的建筑物带给人一种平和、快乐的感觉。他的许多设计都带有水池、花卉，还安有屋顶天窗，好让光线进来。他设计建筑物通常以带给人愉悦为宗旨，力图为人们创造一个空间，一个远离都市生活那种繁忙格调的空间。

山崎实在几家公司供过职，但是，他的成功却始于他开办自己的公司。1956年，他因所设计的密苏里圣路易斯机场而荣获建筑家一等奖。

---

peace *n.* 和平

roof *n.* 屋顶

First Honor Award for his design of an airport in St. Louis, Missouri. He won two more awards over the next five years. In 1962, he designed the World Trade Center in New York. It is very famous.

In 1993, a bomb *exploded* in the World Trade Center. But the buildings did not fall down because they had a good design. (Sadly, in 2001 two planes crashed into the World Trade Center and the building fell.)

Yamasaki had strong opinions about his buildings. They had to be built his way. He refused to change the design of his buildings, *even if* he lost a job.

Minoru Yamasaki died in 1986. He designed more than 300 buildings. People will enjoy the design and beauty of his buildings for a very long time.

随后5年里，他又赢得了两项奖。1962年，他设计了纽约市的世界贸易中心。这是一处非常著名的建筑物。

1993年，一颗炸弹在世界贸易中心爆炸，但这处建筑群却没有被炸毁，因为它的设计非常可靠、合理。（本书编者注：遗憾的是，世界贸易中心的两幢高层建筑于2001年9月11日又一次成为恐怖分子袭击的主要目标，遭巨型飞机撞击后坍塌。）

山崎实对自己所设计的建筑物态度执着，要求人们必须按他的方式建造，拒绝改变其建筑物的设计，即使丢了饭碗也在所不惜。

山崎实于1986年谢世。他一生设计的建筑超过300幢。人们将可长久地鉴赏他建筑物中的绝妙设计与惊人之美。

---

explode *v.* 爆炸   even if 即使

Akio Morita

Akio Morita was born in 1921 in Nagoya, Japan. For 14 *generations*, his family owned a company that made a rice drink called *sake*. His family wanted him to work in their business. But Akio wanted to have his own business.

He and his partner, Masaru Ibuka, started the Sony company. It is one of the most successful companies in the world.

盛田昭夫

盛田昭夫1921年出生于日本名古屋。他家拥有一份祖传14代的家业——酿制一种叫作"清酒"的米酒公司。家里想要他继承家业。但是,昭夫想开办自己的公司。他和搭档井深大创建了索尼公司——世界上最成功的公司之一。

generation　n. 代；一代　　　　　　　　　　　　　sake　n. 清酒

Morita had some ideas that were new to business. They were not *typical*. First, he wanted people to think of quality when they heard the name Sony. Second, he wanted to make Zand sell his products around the world. Morita and his partner created many new products. In 1957, Sony produced a very small radio. It was so small that it fit in a pocket. Next, they made an eight-inch television and a videotape recorder. Years later, Morita decided to create a small tape recorder. It was *portable*. People could carry it with them and listen to music. The tape recorder also had headphones. He called it the Walkman. All of these products were very popular. They were also very good. After a while, people started to buy Sony products because of the high quality. Morita's idea worked!

盛田在经营业务上有独到见解，虽然那些见解在当时尚不具有典型性。首先，他想要人们一听到索尼这个名字就联想起质量这个概念。其二，他想要在全世界范围内制造和销售他的产品。盛田和他的搭档开发了许多新的产品。1957年，索尼公司推出一种微型收音机，小到能把它放到口袋里。接着，他们又上市一种8英寸的电视机和一种磁带录像机。几年以后，盛田决定要制造一种小型磁带录音机，要小巧方便，人们可以随身携带和听音乐。录音机上还带耳机。他把收录机叫作"随身听"。所有这些产品都非常畅销，而且质量上乘。不久，人们因其质量优良，纷纷购买索尼产品。盛田的经营理念成功了！

---

typical *adj.* 典型的   portable *adj.* 轻便的

In 1963, Morita and his family moved to the United States. He wanted to understand the American way of life. Then he could make products that Americans liked. His plans worked again. Sony became the most popular brand in the United States.

Morita was a *brilliant* businessman. People started to call him "Mr. Sony." He traveled around the world and met world leaders and businesspeople. He worked very hard. He also enjoyed other activities. He went to plays and concerts. He gave big parties and attended important events. He loved to play sports. Even in his sixties, he learned new sports. He liked to water ski and play tennis. Akio Morita lived a very full life. He died at the age of 78. He worked hard, and he saw many of his dreams *come true*.

1963年，盛田举家移居美国。他想要理解美国式的生活方式，以便能制造出让美国人倾心的产品。他的计划又一次成功了，索尼成为美国最流行的品牌。

盛田是一位杰出的企业家。人们开始称呼他"索尼先生"。他周游世界各地，与世界各国领袖和商界要人会面。他工作非常努力，同时也爱好其他活动。他去看戏，听音乐会，举行盛大的宴会，也参与重大活动。他喜爱体育运动，年过花甲，还学练新的运动项目，他喜欢滑水和打网球。盛田昭夫过着充实的生活。他78岁辞世。他一生勤奋努力，亲眼看见了自己的许多梦想——成真。

---

brilliant *adj.* 杰出的

come true 实现

15

Maria Callas

Maria Callas was born Maria Anna Sofia Cecilia Kalogeropoulus in New York City in 1923. Her parents were from Greece. Her mother wanted her children to study music. When Maria was seven and her sister was 13, they began singing and piano lessons.

Maria had a beautiful voice but she was very shy. Her mother *forced* her daughter to sing at contests and on radio programs. Maria won many top prizes, but she wasn't very happy.

Maria's father did not want to pay for *expensive* music lessons. He and his wife argued. When Maria was 13, she moved to Greece with

---

玛丽亚·卡拉斯

玛丽亚·卡拉斯1923年出生于纽约市，原名玛丽亚·安娜·索菲亚·西西利亚·卡拉格罗普路丝，祖籍希腊。母亲想要孩子们学习音乐，因此在玛丽亚7岁、姐姐13岁时，她们就开始上声乐和钢琴课了。

玛丽亚虽然嗓音甜美，却非常害羞。她的母亲逼着她去参加歌唱比赛和电台的音乐节目，尽管玛丽亚获得了许多头等奖，却并不特别开心。

玛丽亚的父亲不想支付昂贵的音乐课学费，就和妻子三天两头地吵架。玛丽亚13岁时，她随母亲及姐姐移居希腊。母亲谎报了玛丽亚的实

---

force *v.* 促使；强迫

expensive *adj.* 昂贵的

her mother and sister. Her mother lied about Maria's age and got her into the Athens Conservatory. Maria studied hard for two years. She had no time for friends or fun.

In 1939, Maria began to study with a world-famous Spanish *opera* singer, Elvira de Hidalgo. She changed Maria's life. De Hidalgo taught her to sing and act. She also taught her how to fix her hair and choose beautiful clothes. Maria joined Greece's National Opera at age 16 and took the stage name Maria Callas. At 17, she was a *permanent* member. She was the youngest person ever to join a European opera company.

际年龄，让她进入了雅典音乐学院。玛丽亚在那儿艰苦学习了两年，既没有时间交朋友，也没有时间玩。

1939年，玛丽亚开始师从一位世界著名的西班牙歌剧演唱家埃尔维拉·德·伊达尔戈。她改变了玛丽亚的一生。德·伊达尔戈教她唱歌和演戏，还教她怎样梳理头发，怎样挑选漂亮衣服。16岁时，玛丽亚加入了希腊国家歌剧院，舞台艺名为玛丽亚·卡拉斯。17岁时，她成为剧院的终身演员，是加入欧洲歌剧公司的成员中年龄最小的一位。

---

opera *n.* 歌剧　　　　　　　　　　　permanent *adj.* 永久的

Soon Callas became an *international* star. Some called her the "Golden Voice of the Century". She acted and sang with great *emotion*. Her style changed opera forever. In 1947, she joined La Scala, the leading opera house in Milan. By age 24, Callas was giving 50 performances a year. Some people said this was not good for her singing voice.

Sadly, Callas was not happy. She argued with everyone and did not get along with other singers. She had a problem with her throat and started to lose her singing voice when she was only 35. She divorced her husband to be with her boyfriend, the millionaire Aristotle Onassis. But Onassis did not marry her. He married Jacqueline Kennedy. Maria Callas died in 1977 at the age of 53. We remember her as one of the greatest opera singers of the twentieth century.

卡拉斯很快成了国际明星。有些人称她为"世纪金嗓子"。她的表演和歌唱充满激情，她的风格从此一改歌剧的演唱形式。1947年，她加入了拉·斯卡拉——意大利米兰的头等歌剧院。到24岁时，卡拉斯每年表演达50场。有人提醒说，这样唱下去对嗓子不利。

遗憾的是，卡拉斯还是不开心。她跟谁都会吵起来，与别的歌手相处得并不融洽。她的喉咙也出现了问题，年仅35岁就开始失声。她为了和男朋友——百万富翁亚里士多德·奥纳西斯在一起，与丈夫离了婚，但奥纳西斯并没有娶她，而是与杰奎琳·肯尼迪结婚了。1977年，玛丽亚·卡拉斯去世，终年53岁。我们纪念她，推崇她为20世纪最伟大的歌剧演唱家之一。

---

international *adj.* 国际的   emotion *n.* 情绪

16

Cesar Chavez

César Chávez was born in 1927 near Yuma, Arizona. His family owned a farm, but they did not have enough money to stay on the farm. So when César was 11, the family moved to California. They traveled to many farms to find work.

The Chávez family lived in work *camps*. The camps were *terrible*

克萨·查维斯

克萨·查维斯1927年出生于亚利桑那州的尤马县附近。他家有一个农场，但微薄的家底维持不了农场的花销。于是在克萨11岁时，他们一家搬到了加利福尼亚，曾去过许多农场找活干。

查维斯一家住在工作营地里。 营地是很糟糕的地方，经常没有水

camp *n.* 营地   terrible *adj.* 糟糕的

places. Often they did not have water for drinking and bathing. Often the family lived in a one-room house. Other times they stayed in a *tent*. They worked many hours in the fields. Sometimes the farmers cheated them. They paid the workers very little money. Most of the workers were from Mexico and did not speak English. They were afraid to say anything about the low pay because they did not want to lose their jobs.

Chávez saw these problems, and he did not forget them. He was intelligent. But he did not have much education. His family moved so often that sometimes he went to a school for only a week. Sometimes he went for only a day. He went to over 65 schools before he finished eighth grade.

Chávez was in the *navy* during World War II. After the war, he got married and got a job on a farm. There were problems on this farm,

---

喝，没有水洗澡。一家人通常挤在一间房子里住，有时还只能待在帐篷里。他们在地里一干就是好多个小时，有时农场主还欺骗他们，只付给工人微薄的薪水。大部分工人来自墨西哥，不会说英语。他们不想丢掉饭碗，所以也不敢提起低薪之事。

　　查维斯看到了这些问题，就暗记在心里。他天资聪颖，可惜没受过什么教育。他家频繁地搬迁，使得他有时去学校刚上一周课就又得挪地方，有时甚至只上了一天课就得走。在读完八年级时，他就去过不下65所学校。

　　第二次世界大战时，查维斯参加了海军。战后，他结了婚，在农场谋了一份工作。这个农场也存在不少问题，查维斯和工人们谈到他们应有的

---

tent　*n.*　帐篷　　　　　　　　　　　　　　　navy　*n.*　海军

too. Chavéz talked to the workers about their rights. The owners got mad, and Cháez's boss fired him. Chávez began to work for a group that helped Mexican Americans have better lives. Then he started a farm workers' *union*.

Chávez became famous because of his ideas. Chávez did not like *violence*. He helped workers in peaceful ways. Often he fasted. When he fasted, people noticed him, and then they talked about the workers' problems, too. The government eventually passed laws to protect workers and make their living and working conditions better.

Chávez died in 1993 at the age of 66. He had health problems because he worked hard and fasted for many years. He gave his life to help others. César Chávez was a great hero in the fight for equal rights.

权利，把农场主气得大发雷霆。查维斯的老板解雇了他，他从此开始效力于另一组织，帮助墨西哥裔美国人争取更好的生活，其后他还创建了农场工人工会。

查维斯因其思想观念而闻名。他并不喜欢暴力，而是帮助工人用和平的方式做斗争。他经常绝食。他一绝食，人们就会关注他，顺便也会谈起工人的状况。最终，政府通过了法律来保护工人，使他们的生活及工作条件得到改善。

查维斯死于1993年，享年66岁。他工作拼命，绝食多年，因而疲劳成疾。他毕生帮助他人，是为平等权利而奋斗的伟大英雄。

---

union *n.* 工会   violence *n.* 暴力

17

Anne Frank

Anne Frank was born in 1929 in Frankfurt, Germany. Her family was *Jewish*. She lived happily with her parents and older sister, Margot. In 1933, Adolf Hitler became the *leader* of Germany. Then everything changed.

Hitler passed laws against Jews

安妮·法兰克

安妮·法兰克1929年出生于德国的法兰克福，家族属犹太血统。她和父母及姐姐玛格特一起原本过着快乐的生活。1933年，阿道夫·希特勒成为德国元首，此后一切都变了。

希特勒通过法令反对犹太人和其他种族的人。这些人丢了工作，被迫

Jewish *adj.* 犹太族的　　　　　　　　　　　leader *n.* 元首

and other groups of people. They lost their jobs and were forced out of their homes. Many people were killed. The government sent others to prisons called concentration camps. Life in the camps was *horrible*. Millions of people died there.

The Frank family ran away to Amsterdam, Holland. They were safe for a while. In 1939, World War II started, and in 1940, Hitler's army came to Holland. Life became very bad in Holland, too.

Anne's father, Otto, hid his family in secret rooms in an office building. Another Jewish family hid there, too. Dutch friends brought food for them. Often they did not have enough food. During the day, they had to be very quiet. They lived in fear. They stayed there almost two years.

Every day Anne Frank wrote in her *diary*. She described her

离开自己的家。许多人被杀害了，另一些人则被政府送到一种叫作集中营的监狱里。集中营里的生活令人毛骨悚然，数以百万计的人们死在那里。

法兰克一家逃到荷兰的阿姆斯特丹，暂时安全了一阵子。1939年，第二次世界大战爆发，1940年，希特勒的军队开进荷兰，于是她们在荷兰的日子也变得难熬起来。

安妮的父亲奥托把全家藏在一幢办公大楼的秘密房间里，另一家犹太人也藏在那里。荷兰朋友为他们捎来食品维持生命，但通常食物都不够吃。白天，他们得非常安静，不出声，每天生活在恐惧之中。就这样，他们在那里藏匿了差不多两年。

安妮·法兰克把每天的事都写进了日记，描述她的感受，记下所目

---

horrible *adj.* 可怕的   diary *n.* 日记

feelings and what she saw. Life was very hard, but she wrote about good things, too. On June 6, 1944, the two families heard important news on their radio. The armies of England and the United States were now in France. The war was going to end. Everyone was very happy.

Right before the war ended, someone *betrayed* them. The German secret police came. The police sent the two families to the concentration camps. Sadly, they were on the last train from Amsterdam to the concentration camps.

Anne's mother died of starvation. Anne and her sister died from a disease called *typhus*. Only Otto Frank survived. In 1948, he published *The Diary of Anne Frank*. Because of her diary, people all over the world know the story of Anne Frank.

睹的一切。生活很艰难，但是她仍然写下了一些美好的事情。1944年6月6日，这两个犹太家庭从收音机里听到了重要消息：英美军队现已到达法国，战争即将结束。每个人都感到非常欢欣鼓舞。

就在战争即将结束之时，有人背叛了他们。德国秘密警察来了，把两家人送到了集中营。很不幸，他们被押上了从阿姆斯特丹去集中营的最后一趟列车。

安妮的母亲死于饥饿，安妮和她的姐姐死于斑疹伤寒症，只有奥托·法兰克幸存下来。1948年，他出版了《安妮·法兰克日记》。这本日记让全世界的人都知道了安妮·法兰克的故事。

---

betray *v.* 背叛

typhus *n.* 斑疹伤寒症

18

Roberto **C**lemente

Roberto Clemente was born in 1934 near San Juan, Puerto Rico. His parents did not have much money. But they taught their children to be good and honest. They also taught their children the importance of *honor*. Clemente had all of these *qualities*.

罗伯特·克莱门特

罗伯特·克莱门特1934年出生于波多黎各的圣胡安市。他的父母虽不富有，但一向教导孩子们做人要正派、诚实，还教育孩子们要珍视名誉。克莱门特在这些方面都不负所望，兼具了这些良好的品质。

honor *n.* 名誉　　　　　　　　　　　　　quality *n.* 品质

As a child, Roberto loved baseball. He listened to baseball games on the radio. He played baseball with his friends. He also played in high school on a city team. When he graduated from high school in 1953, nine *professional* teams wanted Clemente to play for them. The Brooklyn Dodgers offered him $10,000. Clemente said "yes." Then another team offered him $30,000! Clemente asked his parents for advice. His mother said that he must keep his word. So he signed a *contract* with the Dodgers. But he never played a game with them.

In 1954, he began to play for another team, the Pittsburgh Pirates. The Pirates were not winning a lot of games. But Clemente helped them get better. In 1960, the Pirates won the World Series Championship for the first time in 33 years. In 1965, Clemente won the award for the Most Valuable Player. In 1971, the Pirates won the

孩提时代，罗伯特就热爱棒球。他从收音机里收听棒球比赛节目，和朋友们一起打棒球，上中学时，还打进了该市的棒球队。1953年从中学毕业后，有9支职业球队想邀他加盟。纽约布鲁克林区的道奇斯队给他提供了一万美元的佣金。克莱门特答应说："好。"然后另一支球队竟提出给他三万美金！克莱门特于是征求父母的意见。他母亲提醒他必须遵守诺言。因此，他还是与道奇斯队签了合同，不过他却未曾和他们一起打过任何比赛。

1954年，他开始效力于另一支球队，即匹兹堡海盗队。海盗队赢球不多，但克莱门特帮助他们取得了较好的战绩。1960年，海盗队赢得了33年来第一次世界锦标赛的冠军。1965年，克莱门特获得"最有价值选

professional *adj.* 专业的   contract *n.* 合同

World Series again. Clemente was named the Most Valuable Player in the series.

Clemente received many awards and made a lot of money. But he gave a lot, too. He gave to charities in the United States and in Puerto Rico. Every winter he went back to Puerto Rico and worked with children. He taught them about baseball. He also taught them about honor and honesty.

In December 1972, there was an *earthquake* in Nicaragua. Clemente collected food, clothing, and medicine for the people. On New Year's Eve, he went on a plane to bring the supplies to Nicaragua. But after the plane took off, it *crashed* into the water. Everyone on the plane died. Roberto Clemente was a great baseball player and a hero.

手"奖。1971年，海盗队再次赢得世界锦标赛冠军。克莱门特在锦标赛中被推举为"最有价值选手"。

克莱门特一生获得过许多奖项，赚了许多钱，但也捐赠出了许多。他向美国和波多黎各的慈善机构都提供过捐赠。每年冬天，他还返回波多黎各和孩子们待在一起，教他们棒球知识，教他们热爱名誉，信守诚实。

1972年12月，尼加拉瓜发生地震。克莱门特为受灾的人们募集食品、衣服和药物。新年除夕，他乘飞机给尼加拉瓜运送供给品。但是，飞机起飞后失事坠落水中，飞机上的乘客全部遇难。罗伯托·克莱门特不仅是一位伟大的棒球运动员，同时也是一位伟大的英雄。

---

earthquake *n.* 地震　　　　　　　　　　　crash *v.* 撞击；坠毁

19

Jane Goodall

Jane Goodall was born in 1934 in London, England. When she was two years old, her father gave her a toy *chimpanzee* named Jubilee. It was her favorite toy. In fact, she still has Jubilee at her home in England. She also loved to play with animals and read stories. Her favorite stories were about *Africa*. Her childhood dream was to go there.

珍·古道尔

珍·古道尔1934年出生于英国伦敦。两岁时，父亲送给她一个名叫朱比利的玩具猩猩，这是她最喜欢的玩具。事实上，她至今在英国的家中还保留着这个朱比利。她还喜欢和动物一起玩耍，喜欢读故事书。她最喜欢有关非洲的故事；儿时就梦想去非洲。

chimpanzee *n.* 黑猩猩   Africa *n.* 非洲

Jane went to *secretarial* school and then she worked for a film company. A friend invited her to Kenya, so she worked as a waitress and saved enough money for the boat trip to Kenya. She was 23 years old.

In Kenya, she met the famous *anthropologist* Louis Leakey. Goodall knew so much about Africa that Leakey hired her as his assistant. She traveled with him and his wife, Mary, to search for evidence of prehistoric man. Leakey and Goodall wanted to study chimpanzees because they were very similar to humans. Goodall did not have a university degree. But Leakey thought she was the ideal person to study chimpanzees.

At first the government did not approve of Goodall's work. It was unusual for a woman to live in the wild country alone. Her mother decided to go with her, so the government finally agreed.

珍后来读了秘书学校，然后去了一家胶片公司工作。一个朋友邀她去肯尼亚，于是她去当女招待，攒足了从水路去肯尼亚的费用。那年她23岁。

在肯尼亚，她遇到了著名的人类学家路易斯·利基。古道尔对非洲了解颇多，于是利基雇她当自己的助手。她与利基和利基的妻子玛丽一起去寻找史前人类的证据。利基和古道尔打算先研究黑猩猩，因为黑猩猩和人类非常相似。尽管古道尔没有大学学历，但利基认为她是研究猩猩的最理想人选。

开始，政府没有同意古道尔的工作，因为一个女子只身在荒野的国度生活可非同一般。她的母亲后来决定与她同行，政府最终还是同意了。

---

secretarial *adj.* 秘书的   anthropologist *n.* 人类学家

In July 1960, Goodall began to study the chimpanzees. It wasn't easy at first. Every morning she went to the same place. After about six months, the chimps came near her. She gave each one a name, like a person. Goodall was the first scientist to do this. She thought that each chimpanzee had its own *personality*, just like people. One day, she noticed that the chimpanzees used tools to get their food. Scientists always thought only people knew how to use tools! She also discovered that chimps eat meat as well as fruit and plants.

Goodall was married twice. She also has a son. Her first husband was a *photographer*, and her second husband was the Director of National Parks. Both men shared Goodall's love of Africa and animals.

Goodall studied chimpanzees for over 40 years. She changed the way scientists study animals. Today she travels the world and talks about the importance of chimpanzees.

1960年7月，古道尔开始研究猩猩。开头很艰难，每天早上她都要去同一个地方守候，6个月后，猩猩与她亲近了。就像给人取名一样，她给每只猩猩都取了个名字。古道尔是第一个这样做的科学家。她认为猩猩就像人一样，每只都有自己的个性。有一天，她注意到猩猩在使用工具获取食物，而科学家们一直认为只有人类才懂得怎样使用工具！她还发现猩猩除了吃水果和植物外，也吃肉。

古道尔结过两次婚，有一个儿子。她的第一个丈夫是位摄影师，第二个是国家公园的经理。这两个男人和古道尔一样，都热爱非洲和动物。

古道尔研究了四十多年猩猩，她改变了科学家研究动物的方式。如今，她周游世界，宣传猩猩的重要性。

---

personality n. 个性　　　　　　　　photographer n. 摄影师

Pele

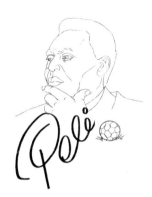

One of the greatest soccer players of all time is Pelé. He was born Edson Arantes do Nascimento in 1940 in Três Corações, Brazil. His first soccer ball was a *grapefruit*. He also used an old *sock* and filled it with newspaper. Pelé left school at a young age to play soccer

贝利

贝利是有史以来最伟大的足球运动员之一。1940年他出生在巴西的特瑞斯·可拉可斯，原名艾迪逊·阿兰蒂斯·德·纳西曼托。他的第一个足球是一个葡萄柚。他还把报纸塞在一只旧短袜里当足球踢。贝利年龄很小就辍学去踢球，并打工以补贴家用，后来才修完中学和大学的课程。

grapefruit *n.* 葡萄柚　　　　　　　　　　　　　　　sock *n.* 短袜

and work to help his family. Later in life, he finished high school and college.

Pelé was only 17 when people started to talk about him. It was 1958. Brazil was playing in the World Cup soccer *competition*. Pelé had an *injury*. He didn't play the first games, but his team needed him. Then Pelé went on the field. Pelé scored the only goal of the last game, and Brazil won the World Cup.

Pelé played professional soccer for 22 years. He scored 1,281 goals—more goals than any other player in the world. He helped Brazil win three World Cup titles. Pelé retired from soccer in 1971. People all over the world admired Pelé. Presidents and world leaders invited him to their countries. Nigeria once stopped its war for three

---

　　贝利17岁时，人们就开始谈论他。那是在1958年，巴西队打入了世界杯足球决赛。贝利当时受了伤，没有参加第一轮比赛。但球队需要他，于是贝利又出现在足球场上，并且踢进了最后一场比赛的唯一一个球，使巴西队赢得了世界杯的冠军。

　　贝利踢了22年的职业足球，共进球1281个——比世界上任何其他球员进的球都多。他帮助巴西队3次赢得世界杯的称号。1971年，贝利从足球场上退役。全世界的人们都敬佩贝利，各国总统和世界要人都邀请他去

---

competition *n.* 比赛   injury *n.* 伤害

days to let Pelé play. His talent is very unusual. Doctors once tested Pelé to find out why he played soccer so well. They found that he had excellent eyesight. He is also very intelligent. Pelé liked to do math problems and play *chess*. He said these activities helped him play better.

Pelé is married and has three children. He likes to be with his family. He also plays the guitar and writes songs. Pelé cares about people, especially children. He gives money to help poor children. He never *advertises* for tobacco or liquor companies. He knows that he has a great influence on young people. Pelé once said that he wants to "unite people, never to separate them." He is loved and admired all over the world.

访问他们的国家。尼日利亚曾经停战三天，好让贝利在那里一展球技。他的才能非同一般。医生曾测试过贝利，以期望找出为什么他球踢得这么好的原因。他们发现，他的视力非常好，而且非常聪明。贝利喜欢做数学题目和下象棋，他说这些活动有助于他把球踢得更好。

贝利结了婚，有3个孩子。他喜欢和家人待在一起，还喜欢弹吉他、写歌。贝利关心他人，尤其是小孩子。他捐钱帮助贫穷的孩子，而且从不给烟草或酒类公司做广告，因为他知道自己对年轻人很有影响力。贝利曾经说过，他要"团结人民，永不分离"。他是广受全世界爱戴和敬慕的人。

---

chess *n.* 象棋   advertise *v.* 为……做广告

21

Muhammad Ali

In 1954, a shy boy named Cassius Clay, Jr., learned to *box* at a *gym* in Louisville, Kentucky. He was only 12 years old. At the gym, he met a trainer who taught him to move with light, quick steps. Cassius had a natural talent for boxing. With his skills and good training, he quickly became a champion.

穆罕默德·阿里

1954年，一个名叫小卡修斯·克莱的羞涩男孩在肯塔基州路易斯维尔市的一个体育馆学习拳击，那时他才12岁。在体育馆里，他碰到一位教练，教他用轻快、敏捷的步子移动身体。卡修斯很有拳击天赋，他的娴熟技艺和受到的良好训练使他很快就在拳坛夺冠。

box *v.* 拳击；打拳   gym *n.* 体育馆

In 1959, Clay won the National Golden Gloves title. The next year, he won an Olympic gold medal and became a professional boxer. Clay believed in himself. His famous words were "I am the greatest!" He told everyone that he was going to be *champion* of the world. Cassius Clay got a lot of attention. He wanted to use his fame to help get more rights for African-Americans.

In 1964, Clay became heavyweight champion of the world. Then he changed his faith and became a Muslim. He also changed his name to Muhammad Ali. In 1967, Ali refused to go into the army and fight in the Vietnam War. He said his reasons were *religious*. The World Boxing Association took away his title. They said that he could not box in the United States again.

1959年，克莱赢得"全国金手套"的称号。第二年，他赢得奥林匹克金牌，并成为一名职业拳击手。克莱相信自己。他的名言就是："我是最好的！"他告诉每个人说，他要成为世界冠军。这样一来，卡修斯·克莱的大名一下子备受关注。而他是想利用他的声望为非洲裔美国人获得更多权利。

1964年，克莱成为世界重量级拳击冠军。之后，他改变信仰，成为一名穆斯林，同时更名为穆罕默德·阿里。1967年，阿里拒绝参军去越南作战，并解释说是出于宗教的原因才这么做的。世界拳击协会为此取消了他的称号。他们声称，阿里再也不能在美国打拳击了。

---

champion *n.* 冠军

religious *adj.* 宗教的

Years later, the people in the *association* changed their minds. They allowed him to come back to fight in the ring. In 1974, Ali became champion again. He was the only man to be champion three times. Everyone in the world knew about Muhammad Ali. Everyone agreed that Ali was the greatest.

Eventually, Ali began to slow down. He lost his title to other boxers. In the 1980s, Ali told the world that he had a brain disease called Parkinson's disease. Now it is hard for him to speak and to use his arms and legs. But he still works for many *charities*. Ali likes to help young people in his town. He also travels all over the world to talk about human rights. He is a true hero of his time.

几年后，协会成员回心转意，允许他重新回到拳击赛场。1974年，阿里再次成为冠军。他是唯一夺得三次冠军的拳击手，从此穆罕默德·阿里誉满天下。每个人都赞同，阿里是最棒的。

后来，阿里开始走下坡路，把曾经赢得的称号拱手让给了别的选手。20世纪80年代，阿里向世界宣告，他得了帕金森氏脑部疾病。现在，他说话困难，手脚不便。但仍坚持为许多慈善机构服务。阿里喜欢帮助镇上的年轻人，还周游世界，宣扬人权。他是一位真正的时代英雄。

---

association *n.* 协会

charity *n.* 慈善

22

Anita Roddick

Anita Roddick was always different. She didn't follow everyone else. She had her own ideas. When she was in high school, she wanted to wear makeup. But she did not have money. So Anita used ashes as eye color. She used *mayonnaise* to make her hair shine. Anita made *cosmetics* from natural things. Later on, she did it again. Only this time it made her rich!

安妮塔·罗迪克

安妮塔·罗迪克总是与众不同，从来不步他人后尘，她有自己的主见。在上中学时，她想化妆，却没有钱买化妆品。于是，安妮塔就用灰末做眼影，用蛋黄酱润泽头发，利用天然材料调制化妆品。后来，她又重操旧业，不过这次却令她财源广进。

---

mayonnaise *n.* 蛋黄酱　　　　　　　　　　cosmetic *n.* 化妆品

She was born Anita Perella in 1944 in Littlehampton, England. Anita became a teacher and taught for a year. Then she worked for the United Nations and traveled around the world. In 1970, she married Gordon Roddick. They had two children. Gordon also loved to travel. He decided that he wanted to ride a horse from Argentina to New York. Anita Roddick needed money while he was away. She decided to open a cosmetics shop.

Roddick found a shop in Brighton, England. The rent was very cheap. The store smelled and the roof *leaked*. Anita washed the walls many times. But they were still damp and green. They still smelled, too. So she painted the walls green. She filled the shop with flowers and *perfume*. She called it The Body Shop. It opened March 27, 1976.

　　1944年，她出生于英格兰的小汉普敦，原名安妮塔·佩蕾拉。后来，安妮塔当了一名教师，教了一年书。然后，她就职于联合国，跑遍世界各地。1970年，她嫁给了戈登·罗迪克，有了两个孩子。戈登也喜欢旅游，还打算从阿根廷一直骑马到纽约。他远行在外时，安妮塔·罗迪克需要钱，于是就决定开一家化妆品店。

　　罗迪克在英国的布赖敦找到一家店铺，租金非常便宜，但房里气味难闻，屋顶还漏水。安妮塔反反复复地洗刷墙壁，但墙壁还是潮湿不堪，绿霉点点，气味难除。于是，她就把墙壁漆成绿色，在店里喷洒了香水，摆满了鲜花，把店铺取名为美体商店。1976年3月27日，商店开张了。

---

leak *v.* 漏　　　　　　　　　　　　　　perfume *n.* 香水

Roddick made the cosmetics herself. She used *ingredients* such as plants, honey, *cucumber*, and other natural things. She also poured strawberry oil in front of her shop so people would follow the smell into her store. They did. People loved her products. The shop was a big success. Soon Roddick opened another shop. It was painted green, of course.

A year later, Gordon Roddick returned home. The Roddicks worked day and night, and the two shops were very successful. Anita Roddick traveled to many different countries. She talked to women about health and beauty. She used many of their ideas in her cosmetics. Soon, The Body Shop had stores all over the world. Maybe there's one near you.

罗迪克自己制作化妆品，她使用的原料有草本植物、蜂蜜、黄瓜，还有其他天然原料。她还把草莓油泼洒到店前，好让人们追循着香味来到店里。他们果然这么来了。人们喜爱她的产品，生意做成功了。很快，罗迪克又开了一家店铺。当然，这家店铺也漆成了绿色。

一年后，戈登·罗迪克回到了家。夫妇俩起早贪黑，把两家店铺都经营得非常出色。安妮塔·罗迪克还去过许多国家，与女性朋友谈论保健与美容，把她们的许多想法都融入她的化妆产品中。很快，美体商店在全世界都有了分店。也许，在你附近就有那么一家。

---

ingredient *n.* 原料

cucumber *n.* 黄瓜

23

Princess Diana

Princess Diana

Princess Diana was born Diana Spencer in 1961 in Norfolk, England. She was the daughter of an aristocratic family. Her parents got *divorced* when she was very young. Then the Spencer children lived with their father. Diana went to a *private* girls' school in Switzerland. She returned to England and worked as a kindergarten teacher. Soon after, she started to date Prince Charles, who was a friend of the Spencer family.

戴安娜王妃

1961年，戴安娜王妃出生在英国诺福克的一个贵族家庭，原名戴安娜·斯潘塞。她很小的时候父母就离异了。其后，斯潘塞家的孩子都和父亲住在一起。戴安娜后来去瑞士一所私人女子学校就读。回国后，成为一名幼儿园教师。不久，她开始与查尔斯王子约会。查尔斯王子当时是斯潘塞家族的朋友。

---

divorced *adj.* 离婚的   private *adj.* 私人的

MCGRAW-HILL

Prince Charles and Diana became *engaged*, and in 1981, they got married. Hundreds of millions of people around the world watched the wedding on television. They had two sons, William and Harry. Princess Diana became the most popular member of the *royal* family. Wherever she went, the press photographed her. She was tall, beautiful, and stylish. Women wanted to look like Princess Diana. She became the most photographed woman in the world.

By 1992, the marriage had difficulties. Princess Diana and Prince Charles separated. In 1995, Diana gave a famous television interview. She talked about her personal life and why she was unhappy. The royal family never talked about personal problems. The interview was unusual, but people liked the princess's honesty. In 1996, Princess Diana and Prince Charles divorced.

查尔斯王子与戴安娜订婚后于1981年结婚，全世界数亿人在电视上观看了结婚盛典。他们共有两个儿子，威廉和哈里。戴安娜王妃成为皇室中最受欢迎的成员，不管她到哪里，记者都会紧跟拍照。她个子高挑，容貌俏丽，打扮入时。女人们纷纷效仿她的穿着打扮。戴安娜成为世界上上镜最多的女性。

到1992年，戴安娜王妃和查尔斯王子的婚姻出现了裂痕，他们分居了。1995年，戴安娜接受了一次举世瞩目的电视采访，谈到了她的私生活以及她不快乐的原因。皇室家族从来不谈论私人问题，因而这次采访非同凡响，但人们喜爱戴安娜王妃的诚实。1996年，戴安娜王妃和查尔斯

---

engaged *adj.* 订婚的   royal *adj.* 皇室的

After the divorce, Diana continued her work to help people. She worked with the poor, with people who had AIDS, and with people who had drug problems. Everyone loved her.

In 1997, Diana had a romance with Dodi al-Fayed, an Egyptian *millionaire*. One evening they were in Paris. Photographers followed their car. The car was going very fast, and it *crashed*. Diana and Dodi died in the accident. It was August 31, 1997. She was only 36 years old. People all over the world were very sad about Princess Diana's death. They will always remember her as the "People's Princess."

王子离婚。

离婚后，戴安娜继续致力于扶助他人的工作，她为穷人、艾滋病患者以及染上毒品的人工作。人人都爱戴她。

1997年，戴安娜和埃及百万富翁多迪·阿法耶兹恋爱了。一天晚上，他们的车在巴黎被记者们跟踪拍摄，于是把车开得飞快，结果翻车了，戴安娜和多迪双双死于车祸。那是1997年8月31日，当时她年仅36岁。全世界的人都为戴安娜王妃之死深感哀痛。人们将永远铭记她——"人民的王妃"。

---

millionaire *n.* 百万富翁

crash *v.* 碰撞

Wang Yani

Wang Yani was born in 1975 in Gongcheng, China. Even as a baby, she loved to draw. She drew lines everywhere. She even drew on the walls! Her father was an artist. Yani wanted to be like him. So she tried to stand like her father as he *painted*. This made him laugh. One day, she painted lines on his

王亚妮

王亚妮1975年出生于中国(广西)恭城。她还是个婴儿时，就爱上了涂涂画画，到处画线条，甚至还在墙上画！她的爸爸是一名画家。亚妮也希望像爸爸那样，因此，爸爸画画时她就学爸爸的站姿，那样子还真令她的父亲觉得好笑。一天，她在爸爸的一幅画上画了很多线

---

paint *v.* （用颜料等）画；绘

painting. She was only two and a half years old, but her father got angry. She cried and said, "I want to paint like you!" Then her father thought about his childhood. He also wanted to draw and paint. But his parents didn't understand. They just got angry. He decided to help his daughter become an artist.

Wang Yani's father gave her paint, *brushes*, and paper. She improved very quickly. Soon her lines became flowers, trees, and animals. Other people liked her work very much. Her pictures were in an art *exhibit* in Shanghai when she was only four years old!

By age six, Yani had made over 4,000 paintings and drawings. She loved to draw animals, especially monkeys and cats. Her pictures had bright colors. They had a special style. They were unique. Her father did not give her art lessons. He even stopped

---

条，虽然当时她仅有两岁半，爸爸却生气了，她于是哭着说："我是想像你那样画画！"这令她爸爸想起了自己的童年时代。小时候他也喜欢画、喜欢描，但是他的父母却不理解他，只是生气而已。想到这里，他决定要帮助女儿成为一名画家。

王亚妮的父亲给她准备了涂料、画笔和画纸。亚妮进步得非常快，不久，她笔下的线条变成了花卉、树木和动物。人们非常喜欢她的作品，年仅4岁时，她的画就已经参加上海的美术展览了。

到6岁时，亚妮已经画了四千多幅画和素描。她喜欢画动物，尤其是猴子和猫。她的画色彩明亮，风格迥然，独一无二。她爸爸没有给她上美术课，甚至还停止了自己的绘画，以免女儿的画受他的影响。他把她带到

---

brush *n.* 画笔   exhibit *n.* 展览

painting his own pictures. He did not want his daughter to paint like him. He took her to parks and zoos to get ideas for her work. When Yani was eight years old, one of her monkey paintings was made into a Chinese *postage stamp*. Later, Yani started to draw *landscapes* and people.

Wang Yani's work was shown in Asia, Europe, and North America. When she was just 14 years old, she became the youngest person to have a one-person show at the Smithsonian Institution in Washington, D.C.

Wang Yani was famous at a young age, but she still has a normal life. Her parents never sold her paintings. So the Wang family lives like everyone else. Wang Yani went to high school and has other interests, like sports and music. But her art is still a great joy in her life.

公园和动物园，让她自己寻找绘画灵感和创作的火花。亚妮8岁时，她的一幅猴子图画已经被印制在中国邮票上了。之后，亚妮开始画风景画和人物画。

王亚妮的作品在亚洲、欧洲和北美都被展出过。她刚14岁，就成为在美国首都华盛顿史密斯森尼博物院举办个人画展的最年轻的画家。

虽然王亚妮很小就出名了，但她仍然过着普通人的生活。她的父母也从未出售过她的画作，因此王家的生活过得和其他人一样，没有什么不同。王亚妮上了中学，同时也有着其他的兴趣爱好，比如运动和音乐，但绘画仍是她生活中的最爱。

---

postage stamp 邮票   landscape *n.* 风景画

Wolfgang Amadeus Mozart

Wolfgang Amadeus Mozart was a musical *genius*. He was born in 1756 in Salzburg, Austria. His father, Leopold, was a musician. He taught Wolfgang and his sister Maria Anna to play musical *instruments*. Wolfgang started to play the piano when he was only three years old. One day, Leopold and some musicians were playing a piece of music. Wolfgang was listening to

乌夫冈·阿马戴乌斯·莫扎特

乌夫冈·阿马戴乌斯·莫扎特是位音乐天才，1756年生于奥地利的萨尔茨堡。他父亲利奥波德是位音乐家。父亲教他和姐姐玛利亚·安娜弹奏乐器。乌夫冈年仅3岁就开始学钢琴。一天，父亲和一些音乐家在弹奏一首曲子，乌夫冈在一旁听着。他们刚一弹完，乌夫冈便把听到的小提琴部分准确地弹奏出来。原来乌夫冈只要听一遍就能记住乐

genius *n.* 天才   instrument *n.* 器具

them. After they finished, he started to play the *violin* part exactly as he had heard it. Wolfgang remembered the music after hearing it just once! Soon Leopold realized that it was impossible to teach his son music because Wolfgang knew almost everything already.

Wolfgang wrote his first piece of music for the piano when he was five years old. When he was six, he was already earning money for his family. He played for kings and queens and other important people. They paid a lot of money to hear him. He wrote his first *symphony* at the age of eight and his first opera at age 11. People called him the "wonder child." Wolfgang liked the attention. He worked hard and traveled a lot, but he was often sick.

Mozart was cute as a child. He had red cheeks and bright, blue eyes. But as he got older, he was not handsome. He was a small man with a large head and pale skin. He was always worried about

---

曲，过耳不忘！不久，他父亲意识到已没有能力再教儿子音乐了，因为乌夫冈几乎已经掌握了父亲所教的一切。

乌夫冈5岁时谱写了第一首钢琴曲，6岁时已经能挣钱养家了。他为国王、王后和权贵们演奏。这些人听他的音乐，给他很高的报酬。乌夫冈8岁时写了第一首交响曲，11岁时写了第一部歌剧。人们称他为"神童"，他也喜欢受到众人的关注。他工作勤奋，喜爱旅游，但经常生病。

莫扎特小时候很可爱，红红的面颊上有一双明亮的蓝眼睛。但他长大后并不英俊，矮小的身材顶着个大脑袋，皮肤苍白。他总是为自己的相貌发愁。莫扎特着装很考究，也特别在意头发，认为这是他的容貌中最漂亮的地方。

---

violin *n.* 小提琴　　　　　　　　　　symphony *n.* 交响乐

his appearance. He liked to wear *elegant* clothes. He also took special care of his hair, which he thought was his best feature.

Mozart fell in love with his landlady's daughter. She did not love him, so he married her sister, Constanze. Constanze was very much like her husband. She was musical and loved to have fun. Unfortunately, the Mozarts had money problems. Wolfgang made a lot of money, but he was always in debt. Sometimes people didn't pay him with money; they gave him watches or jewelry instead. But when he got money, he usually spent it on expensive clothes and *furniture*. One story said that once when Mozart had no money to heat his house, he danced with his wife to keep warm. The Mozarts had six children, but only two lived to be adults.

Mozart worked very hard. He liked to work when it was quiet in the house. He began work at six o'clock in the evening and worked

莫扎特爱上了女房东的女儿，这位姑娘却不喜欢他，因此，莫扎特娶了她的妹妹康斯坦策为妻。她和丈夫非常相像，她也爱好音乐和娱乐活动。不幸的是，莫扎特经济拮据。他钱挣了很多，但总是负债累累。有时，人们并不支付金钱给他做报酬，而是用手表和珠宝饰物代替。他一旦有了钱，就购买华贵的衣服和家具。有人传说，一次，莫扎特没有钱买木柴取暖，便和妻子一起靠跳舞暖身。莫扎特夫妇有6个孩子，但只有两个长大成人。

莫扎特工作非常努力，喜欢在房间里很静的时候工作。他习惯于晚上6点开始创作，通宵达旦。他喜欢站着作曲，经常一宿只睡4个小时。他谱

elegant *adj.* 高雅的　　　　　　　　　　furniture *n.* 家具

all night. He liked to write music while he was standing. He often slept for only four hours a night. He also worked very quickly. He wrote three of his greatest works in only six weeks. He also wrote a whole opera in just a few weeks. Many people believe that Mozart wrote faster than any other composer in history. Mozart also had the *ability* to write all kinds of music. He wrote operas, symphonies, and church music. And he wrote music for every instrument. He even wrote music for clocks. In all, Mozart wrote over 600 pieces of music.

Mozart died at the age of 35. No one really knows how he died. Some people believe someone *poisoned* him. Others say that he had a weak heart. Sadly, no one went to his funeral. They buried him as a poor person in a grave with no name. No one knows where his body is to this day.

曲神速，仅用6周时间，就谱写了他一生中最伟大的三部作品，仅用几周时间，就谱写了一整部歌剧的曲子。许多人认为莫扎特是历史上谱曲最快的作曲家。他还能谱写各种题材的音乐作品。他写歌剧、交响乐和教堂音乐，还为各类乐器写曲，甚至为时钟谱曲。他总共创作了六百多件音乐作品。

　　莫扎特35岁辞世。无人真正知晓他是如何去世的，有人认为他是被别人毒死的，另外一些人则认为是因心脏衰竭而死。可悲的是，无人参加他的葬礼。人们把他当成一个穷人埋在无名墓地，直到今天也无人知道莫扎特的尸骨究竟埋在何处。

---

ability *n.* 能力　　　　　　　　　　　　　poison *v.* 使中毒

26

Dr. James Barry

Dr. James Barry was the first woman in England to go to medical school. When she was growing up, women could not go to medical school. So how did she become a doctor? She simply *pretended* that she was a man.

No one knows Dr. Barry's real name, her birth date, or her family's *background*. Some records show that she was born in 1795 in London. Some people say she was the daughter of a rich man or a royal prince. One fact we know is that in 1810, James Barry became

---

詹姆士·巴里医生

詹姆士·巴里医生是英国第一位进入医学院就读的女性。在她成长的年代里，妇女是不准进入医学院读书的。那么她如何成为一名医生的呢？她索性女扮男装。

没有人知道巴里医生的真实姓名、出生日期及她的家庭背景，只是有些记录表明她于1795年出生在伦敦。有人说，她是一位富豪或者王子的女儿。不过，我们无须怀疑的事实是：巴里于1810年成了爱丁堡大学的一名医科学生。

---

pretend *v.* 假装   background *n.* 背景

a medical student at the University of Edinburgh.

James Barry's classmates made fun of her because she didn't have a beard and she was only five feet tall. But no one thought she was a girl. At the age of 20, James Barry graduated from the University of Edinburgh as a Doctor of Medicine. She was one of the youngest students to complete her studies. Dr. Barry then went to work in a London hospital and studied *surgery*. A year later, she entered the army and became a hospital *assistant*. We will never know how she avoided the army physical exam.

For the next 45 years, Dr. James Barry was a British officer and a successful surgeon. Everyone admired her. She began to do a lot of important work for the army. At that time, England had many colonies around the world. Dr. Barry spent a lot of time in foreign countries. She traveled to India, Corfu, Malta, and Jamaica. In 1856 she went to South Africa, and she was soon known as the

---

　　巴里的同班同学经常拿她开玩笑，因为她没有胡子并且只有5英尺高，但谁也没料到她竟是一位姑娘。20岁时，她作为医学医生从爱丁堡大学毕业，而且是完成学业的最年轻的学生之一。巴里医生毕业后去伦敦一家医院工作并学习外科学，一年后，她参军成了一名医院助理。我们永远无从知晓她是如何避开部队的体检的。

　　后来的45年里，巴里医生成了一名英国军官和成功的外科医生，人人都钦佩她。她为军队做了很多重要的工作。那时，英国在世界上有许多殖民地，巴里医生因此也在国外度过了许多时光。她到过印度、科孚、马耳他和牙买加。1856年她去了南非，很快便成了这个殖民地国家最好的医生和外科大夫。她救过总督的女儿，后来成了总督的私人医生。大家仰慕

---

surgery　*n.*　外科　　　　　　　　　　　　　　assistant　*n.*　助手

best doctor and surgeon in the *colony*. She saved the life of the governor's daughter, and later she became the governor's personal doctor. People admired Dr. Barry, but she also had a *reputation* as a troublemaker. If people talked about her high voice or tiny figure, she became very angry. She was an excellent swordsman, and she started fights often.

Her work also got her in trouble. Dr. Barry wanted the highest medical standards. She made hospitals follow strict rules for taking care of the sick. She reported prison officials if they treated prisoners badly. She made many important changes, but she also made many enemies. Sometimes the army supported her and sometimes it didn't. Once there was even a trial for Dr. Barry because she did not obey orders.

Some people did not agree with Dr. Barry, but they always admired her as a doctor and a surgeon. However, some also thought

---

巴里医生。但她也有个坏名声：爱惹麻烦。一旦人们议论她的尖嗓音和瘦小身材，她就会非常生气。她是个唇枪舌剑的好手，而且常常挑起争端。

她的工作也给她带来了麻烦。巴里医生要求有最高的医疗标准，规定医院护理病人要遵循严格的规章。如果监狱官员虐待犯人，她会告发监狱官员。她锐意改革，因此也树敌不少。军队对她的支持也是反复无常。由于她不服从命令，有一次甚至遭到了审讯。

有些人虽然和巴里医生意见相左，但这些人钦佩她是个好医生、好外科大夫。然而，还是有些人认为这位医生很怪诞，比如她总是闭门着装。其实她常和男军官同住一室，要换衣服就让男军官们离开房间。

---

colony *n.* 殖民地   reputation *n.* 名誉

the doctor was very strange. For example, she always dressed behind closed doors. In fact, she often shared rooms with male officers. She asked them to leave the room when she dressed.

In 1857, at the age of 62, Dr. Barry became Inspector General and moved to Canada. There, she worked to improve the soldiers' living conditions and get better food for them. In 1859, Dr. Barry became ill with the *flu* and went back to England to retire. She was very lonely after that. She died in 1865 at the age of 71.

An army doctor looked at the body quickly and simply said that Dr. Barry was dead. Later, someone discovered she was a woman. The secret was out, but the army never made an official *announcement* about its female officer. They buried Dr. Barry as a man. The details of Dr. Barry's life and the sacrifices she made died with her.

1857年巴里医生62岁时，她被调到加拿大任监察长。在那里，她为改善士兵的生活条件、提高他们的饮食标准做了很多工作。1859年，巴里医生患了流感，退役回到英国。从那以后，她一直孤独地生活着。她于1865年去世，享年71岁。

一位军医快速地查看了巴里的身体，直截了当地说她已去世。尔后，有人发现她竟是一位女性，秘密公开了。但是，军队从未就女军官身份问题发表正式声明，仍将巴里医生作为男子安葬。巴里医生的轶事和自我牺牲的壮举随着她的逝世载入了史册。

---

flu *n.* 流感　　　　　　　　　　　announcement *n.* 声明

27

Charles Dickens

Charles Dickens was born in 1812 in Portsmouth, England. He was the second of eight children. His father always had problems with money. When Charles was 12 years old, his father went to prison because he was

A Charles Dickens Christmas

in *debt*. Charles had to leave school to help his family. He got a job putting labels on bottles of shoe *polish* in a dirty, old factory. Charles

---

查尔斯·狄更斯

查尔斯·狄更斯1812年生于英国的朴次茅斯市，他在8个孩子中排行第二。他父亲经常在经济方面陷入困境，查尔斯12岁时，父亲因负债入狱。查尔斯不得不辍学挣钱，以补贴家用。他在一家又脏又破的老工厂找到一份工作，职责就是把标签贴在鞋油瓶上。查尔斯·狄更斯永远忘不了苦难的童年，他的许多作品都是描写穷人及其艰苦生活的。

---

debt *n.* 债务　　　　　　　　　　　　polish *n.* 擦光剂

Dickens never forgot his difficult childhood. Many of his stories and books were about poor people and their problems.

Later, Charles went back to school for two more years. He left school when he was 15 years old to become a newspaper reporter. In 1836, he began to write *The Pickwick Papers*. It was published as a *series* and was a huge success. By age 24, Dickens was a famous writer in both Great Britain and the United States.

Many people bought his books, but they also paid to hear him read his stories aloud. Because there was no radio or television, people liked to hear famous writers read in public. Dickens read his work like he was acting in a play. He went on very successful reading tours and earned a lot of money.

Dickens was *meticulous*. Everything had to be just right. When

---

后来，查尔斯回到学校又读了两年书。15岁时他离开学校，当了一名报社记者。1836年他开始写连载的系列故事《匹克威克外传》，取得了巨大成功。24岁时，他已经在英国和美国成了著名作家。

许多人买了他的书，还乐意付酬听他朗读书中的故事。那时没有收音机和电视机，人们喜欢听著名作家当众朗诵。狄更斯朗读他的作品时非常投入，就像是入戏表演角色一样。他成功地进行了他的"朗读之旅"，挣了一大笔钱。

狄更斯办事谨慎，追求完美。当他在家里工作时，每件物品都必须各

---

series *n.* 系列　　　　　　　　　　　　meticulous *adj.* 谨慎的

he worked at home, everything had to be in its place. He worked at a desk by a window that always had a vase of flowers and the same ornaments on it. He wrote 2,000 words a day, and he required complete quiet while he wrote. He divided his page into three parts, and on each side he had notes in different colors. The main writing was in the middle, the story notes were in the right margin, and the chapter notes were in the left margin. He also cared a lot about his appearance. Dickens had many mirrors in his home. He combed his hair very often, even at dinner parties! He wore showy clothes, such as red velvet jackets, and he always had many rings on his fingers. He usually looked *overdressed*.

Dickens was *superstitious*. He thought that Fridays were lucky, and

就其位。他的办公桌临窗，窗户前总是摆放着装有鲜花的花瓶和装饰品。狄更斯每天写2 000字，写作时需要绝对安静。他把每页纸分成三部分，每一部分用不同的颜色做笔记。正文写在中间，有关故事的笔记写在右边空白处，章节的要点写在左边空白处。狄更斯很注重仪表，家中有许多面镜子。他非常爱梳理头发，甚至在宴会上也忘不了。他的衣服很花哨，比如身穿红天鹅绒夹克，手上常戴着许多戒指。他看上去总是穿得过于考究。

狄更斯讲迷信。他认为星期五大吉大利；他常触摸某件东西三次，以

---

overdressed *adj.* 穿着过于讲究的   superstitious *adj.* 迷信的

he touched certain things three times for luck. He always slept with his bed in a north-south position. When he spoke in public, he didn't want anyone to sit behind him. Everything around him had to be red, including the table and the *carpet*.

Dickens married Catherine Hogarth in 1836. They did not get along very well, and after 16 years of marriage they separated. Charles and Catherine had 10 children. After the separation, the younger children lived with Charles. Catherine's sister, Georgina, moved in with them and helped Charles manage the house.

Dickens always worked hard. When he was home, he followed a daily *routine*. He got up at seven o'clock, had breakfast at eight, and then worked until two in the afternoon. After that, he had a small lunch and worked or rode his horse until five o'clock. Then he had

---

求好运；他总是要把床摆成坐南朝北的方向才会安然入睡；在公众面前讲话时，他不让任何人坐在他的后面；他周围的一切包括桌子和地毯都必须是红色的。

狄更斯于1836年和凯瑟琳·霍格思结婚。婚后关系一直不太好，16年后，他们离异了。狄更斯和凯瑟琳有10个子女，离异后，年幼些的子女和查尔斯住在一起。凯瑟琳的妹妹乔治娜搬来和他们一起住，帮助查尔斯料理家务。

狄更斯工作非常勤奋。他在家里时日程安排总是极为严格。早上7点钟起床，8点钟用早餐，然后一直工作到下午两点。稍进一点午餐后，再

---

carpet *n.* 地毯　　　　　　　　　　　　routine *n.* 程序；日常工作

supper. After supper, he wrote again or went to the theater. He went to bed at midnight.

Dickens liked to make money. Because of his difficult *childhood*, he was afraid to be poor. In 1867, he began a long reading tour. He traveled throughout Europe and the United States. The trip was very tiring, and he became ill. Two years after he returned home, he died at the age of 58.

Charles Dickens wrote powerful and honest stories about the lives of poor people. The government even passed laws to stop some of the *horrible* things he wrote about in his books. Books like *David Copperfield*, *Great Expectations*, *Oliver Twist*, and *A Christmas Carol* were popular when Dickens wrote them, and they are still popular today.

投入工作或骑马散心直到5点钟。尔后，用晚餐，晚餐后又开始写作或去剧院。午夜时才上床睡觉。

苦难的童年令狄更斯害怕贫穷，他总想着去多挣钱。1867年，他开始了一次长途"朗读之旅"，要穿越整个欧洲和美国。这次旅行使他很劳累，他病倒了，回家两年后去世，享年58岁。

查尔斯·狄更斯写了许多反映贫苦人民真实生活的力作，政府甚至依据他在书中所描写的恐怖之事专门通过法令加以制止。《大卫·科波菲尔》、《远大前程》、《雾都孤儿》和《圣诞欢歌》等在当时就很受百姓喜爱，直到今天仍然十分畅销。

---

childhood *n.* 童年　　　　　　　　　　　　　horrible *adj.* 可怕的

Alfred Nobel

The Nobel Prize is one of the greatest honors in the world today. Once a year, people win this prize for their work in science, medicine, literature, *economics*, or world peace. Each winner receives a gold medal, a *diploma*, and about $1 million. They also earn the respect of

阿尔弗雷德·诺贝尔

诺贝尔奖是当今世界上最伟大的荣誉之一。它一年颁发一次，奖给那些在科学、医学、文学、经济学以及为世界和平事业做出杰出贡献的人士。每位获奖者会得到金牌、证书和约一百万美元奖金，同时受到全世界人民的尊敬。

economics *n.* 经济学   diploma *n.* 证书

people around the world.

Nobel Prize winners receive their awards at ceremonies in Stockholm, Sweden, and Oslo, Norway, on December 10, the *anniversary* of the death of Alfred Nobel. Nobel was a scientist and inventor. In his *will*, he left his fortune to create the Nobel Prize. Nobel wanted people to remember him as a man of peace, but in his lifetime he was most famous for building weapons of war.

Alfred Nobel was born in 1833 in Stockholm, Sweden. His father, Immanuel, was an inventor. After Alfred was born, his father went to Russia to work. He worked with the government and made machinery and explosives. Several years later, Immanuel moved his family to Russia. Alfred and his two older brothers were interested in science and enjoyed watching their father in the laboratory.

When Alfred was 17 years old, he traveled to the United States and several European countries to study. Then he returned to Russia

---

诺贝尔奖得主一般在诺贝尔逝世纪念日——12月10日在瑞典的斯德哥尔摩和挪威的奥斯陆举行的仪式上领奖。诺贝尔是一位科学家和发明家，他留下遗嘱，用他留下的财富设立诺贝尔奖。诺贝尔希望人们记住他是一个爱好和平的人，但是，他的一生却是以制造战争武器而闻名的。

阿尔弗雷德·诺贝尔1833年出生在瑞典的斯德哥尔摩。他的父亲伊曼纽尔是发明家。阿尔弗雷德出生后，他父亲赴俄国工作，为俄国政府制造机械和炸药。几年后，全家移居俄国。阿尔弗雷德和两个哥哥对科学很感兴趣，喜欢观看他们的父亲在实验室工作。

阿尔弗雷德17岁时先后到美国和欧洲的几个国家学习，然后回到俄国和父亲、兄弟们一起工作。他们为俄国军事部门制造火药武器。那时，

---

anniversary *n.* 周年纪念日

will *n.* 遗嘱

to work with his father and his brothers. They worked on *explosive* weapons for the Russian military. At that time, the military used only one type of explosive—gunpowder. Then a chemistry professor showed the Nobels a heavy, oily liquid they could use in their work. It was called *nitroglycerin*. Nitroglycerin was a powerful explosive, but it was dangerous to work with.

Alfred and his father experimented with nitroglycerin. Finally, in 1863, Alfred invented a way to make it more safe. Scientists everywhere praised his work. Nitroglycerin had many good uses. Workers used it to uild roads through mountains and to construct mines deep in the earth.

Nobel's invention was not perfect, however. Nitroglycerin exploded if someone dropped it or used it incorrectly. Sometimes it leaked from the cans. Sometimes workers used the oily liquid on wheels or to clean their shoes! This often caused accidents and

---

军方只用一种型号的火药——黑色火药。后来一位化学教授向他们介绍一种重油性液体用于他们的实验，它叫作硝化甘油。硝化甘油爆炸力很大，使用起来非常危险。

阿尔弗雷德和父亲用硝化甘油做试验，于1863年阿尔弗雷德终于找到了一种更为安全的方法。各地的科学家都称赞他的工作。硝化甘油有许多用途，工人们用它开山筑路以及在地下深处修建矿井。

那时诺贝尔的发明并不完美，硝化甘油一旦摔落在地或操作不当，就会爆炸。有时硝化甘油会从铁罐里渗漏出来，有时工人们还会把这种油性液体用来润滑车轮或用它擦鞋子，因而常常引起伤害事故。不久，因为使用硝化甘油比较危险，一些政府开始禁止使用它。

---

explosive *adj.* 爆炸的　　　　　　　　nitroglycerin *n.* 硝化甘油

injuries. After a while, some governments started to ban nitroglycerin because it was dangerous.

The Nobels continued to experiment to make nitroglycerin safer. Unfortunately, in September 1864, Alfred's brother, Emil, was killed in an explosion in their laboratory. After the accident, Immanuel had a *stroke* and was *paralyzed*. He died eight years later, on the same day Emil had died.

Alfred Nobel wanted to make nitroglycerin safe. He built a new laboratory and continued his work. In 1867, he discovered a new material to mix with the nitroglycerin. This material made the nitroglycerin safer and more effective. He called his new invention "dynamite."

Nobel built factories all over the world. He continued his experiments and developed new and more powerful explosives. He also became interested in weapons. He developed a new type of

---

诺贝尔继续试验，想让硝化甘油更加安全。不幸的是，1864年9月，阿尔弗雷德的兄弟埃米尔在他们的实验室中被炸死。这次事故后，他父亲伊曼纽尔患了中风，瘫痪了，8年后在埃米尔出事的同一个日子里去世。

阿尔弗雷德·诺贝尔想制造安全的硝化甘油。他建造了一个新实验室，继续研究。1867年，他发现把一种新材料与硝化甘油混合，制成的硝化甘油更安全、更有效。他把这种新发明叫作"黄色炸药"。

诺贝尔在世界各地建立工厂，继续做试验，开发出更新、更有威力的炸药。他还对武器产生了兴趣并研制了一种新型的黑色火药以及其他材

---

stroke *n.* 中风

paralyze *v.* 使瘫痪

gunpowder as well as other materials. Nobel became very wealthy. Many people said he was a bad person because he invented destructive weapons. But he believed that nations would stop wars if they had weapons that could destroy each other.

In 1888, Alfred Nobel's older brother, Ludwig, died. A newspaper story *confused* him with Alfred and called him "the *merchant* of death". This upset Alfred very much. He wanted people to remember him as a man of peace. Seven years later he wrote out his will and created the Nobel Prize. When he died in 1896, people called his will the greatest gift ever made by one person. Since 1901, men and women from around the world have received Nobel Prizes for their great achievements. People everywhere now remember Alfred Nobel for his efforts to make the world a better and more peaceful place.

料。诺贝尔变得很富有。许多人说他是个坏人，因为他发明了破坏性武器。而诺贝尔认为，国家与国家有了互相能摧毁对方的武器，他们就会停止战争。

1888年，阿尔弗雷德·诺贝尔的哥哥路德维格去世。一家报纸的报道把他俩混为一谈，并称诺贝尔为"贩卖死亡的商人"，这使得阿尔弗雷德非常气恼。他希望人们记住他是一个爱好和平的人。7年后他写下遗嘱创立了诺贝尔奖。1896年他去世时，人们称他的遗嘱是有史以来的个人最大捐赠。自1901年起，世界各国取得巨大成就的人士均可获得诺贝尔奖。现在全世界人民都记得阿尔弗雷德·诺贝尔为创造一个更美好、更和平的世界所做的努力。

---

confuse *v.* 使混乱；使困惑　　　　　　　　merchant *n.* 商人

29

Sofia Kovalevsky

In the 1800s, women could not go to college and have professions. Women who became doctors, scientists, and businesswomen had to overcome great *obstacles*. Many of these women went against laws, traditions, and the wishes of their families. However, they were dedicated to their work and made great *contributions* to the world. Sofia Kovalevsky was one of these women.

Sofia was born in 1850 in Moscow. Her father was a Russian general. Her mother was the daughter of a well-known mathematician. The family lived in a large mansion near St. Petersburg. Each of them lived in a separate part of the mansion. Her parents were very strict.

索菲亚·科瓦列夫斯基

19世纪，女性不能进大学读书，不能有职业。妇女要想成为医生、科学家或者商人，需要冲破很大的障碍，她们当中许多人要和法律、传统及家庭的意愿抗争。尽管如此，她们仍然致力于工作，为世界做出了巨大的贡献。索菲亚·科瓦列夫斯基就是其中之一。

索菲亚1850年生于莫斯科。父亲是一位俄国将军，母亲是一位著名数学家的女儿。她们家住在圣彼得堡附近，家里人分开居住在一座大楼

---

obstacle *n.* 障碍   contribution *n.* 贡献

Sofia didn't think her parents loved her. She remembered this all of her life.

Sofia Kovalevsky

Sofia loved mathematics at a very early age. When she was 11 years old, she hung up notes from mathematical *lectures* on her walls. She also taught herself physics. A family friend thought Sofia should study mathematics in St. Petersburg. Sofia's father agreed. When she was 15 years old, she went there with her mother and sister.

Sofia and her sister wanted to go to school, but Russian universities didn't *admit* women and their father wouldn't let them study abroad. Sofia's sister thought of a plan. They needed to find a student to marry one of them. The sisters didn't care which one of

里。父母很严厉，以至索菲亚认为父母亲不爱她。对此，她终生难忘。

索菲亚从小就喜欢数学，11岁时就把听数学讲座时记的笔记挂在自己房间的墙上。她还自学了物理学。她们家的一个朋友认为索菲亚应该到圣彼得堡去学习数学，索菲亚的父亲也很赞同。索菲亚15岁时和母亲及姐姐一起去了圣彼得堡。

索菲亚和姐姐想上学，但俄国的大学不允许女子入学，父亲又不让她们出国留学。索菲亚的姐姐想了个主意，她们需要找到一个男生娶她们中的一个为妻。姐妹俩不在乎她们中谁能结婚，也不在乎找个什么样的人。

lecture *n.* 讲座　　　　　　　　　　　　　　admit *v.* 让……进入

them got married. They also didn't care who they found. A student named Vladimir Kovalevsky agreed to their plan. He *promised* to take his new wife to study in Germany. There was one problem. He liked Sofia, but Sofia didn't care about him.

Their father refused to allow the marriage. At that time, younger sisters never married before their older sisters. But Sofia wanted to go to school very much. So, she left a note for her father and went to Kovalevsky's apartment. At that time, a young woman never spent time alone with a young man. Her father had to agree to the marriage to save the family's honor.

The Kovalevskys went to Germany, and Sofia became a mathematics student. They lived apart and *rarely* saw each other. Sofia was very lonely and studied all of the time. In 1871, she moved to Berlin to work with a famous mathematician. Women were not allowed to attend the University of Berlin. The mathematician

---

一个叫作弗拉迪米尔·科瓦列夫斯基的学生同意她们的打算，并承诺可以带新娘去德国学习。不过，有一个问题，他喜欢索菲亚，索菲亚却不喜欢他。

她们的父亲不答应这桩婚事。那时的习俗是，妹妹不能先于姐姐结婚。索菲亚渴望上学，因此，她给父亲留下一张便条，就去了科瓦列夫斯基的住所。那时，年轻女子绝不能单独和青年男子待在一起。为维护家庭声誉，父亲不得不同意这桩婚事。

科瓦列夫斯基夫妇去了德国，索菲亚成了数学系的学生。他们没有住在一起，也很少见面。索菲亚感到很孤独，就把时间全部用在学习上。1871年，她移居柏林跟随一著名数学家学习。当时不允许妇女进柏林大

---

promise *v.* 许诺

rarely *adv.* 很少；难得

was very surprised when she asked him to teach her. He gave her some problems that even his *advanced* students could not solve. When Sofia solved the problems, he accepted her as his student immediately. Three years later, Sofia Kovalevsky received her degree in mathematics.

During these years, Sofia Kovalevsky worked completely alone. She had no social life. Vladimir, her husband, also lived in Berlin, but they lived apart. After five years of friendship, however, they finally fell in love. In 1878, they had a daughter. Kovalevsky stopped studying. She wanted to be a good wife and mother. At last she had love and happiness.

Vladimir taught at the University of Moscow. After a while, he left his teaching job. He began to have money and job problems. Sadly, he lost all of their money and then committed *suicide*. Sofia was devastated.

　　学学习，当她向数学家请教时，数学家感到惊奇。数学家给了她一些高才生也解答不了的难题，让索菲亚去做。当看到索菲亚解决了难题后，数学家马上接受她为学生了。3年后，索菲亚·科瓦列夫斯基获得了数学学位。

　　这些年里，索菲亚·科瓦列夫斯基完全独自学习，没有社交活动。她的丈夫弗拉迪米尔也住在柏林，但他们不住在一起。经过5年的友好交往后，他们终于相爱了，并于1878年生下了一个女儿。科瓦列夫斯基于是停止了学业，她想做个贤妻良母。她终于获得了爱情和幸福。

　　弗拉迪米尔在莫斯科大学教书，可是不久，他失去了教职，开始在经济和工作上遇到麻烦。可悲的是他在财产尽失后自杀了。索菲亚也垮了。

---

advanced *adj.* 先进的；高级的　　　　　　　　　　suicide *n.* 自杀

A great Swedish mathematician helped Kovalevsky get a job as a mathematics professor in Sweden. She became famous because she was the only woman to be a professor in Europe, outside of Italy. In 1888, Kovalevsky competed for the greatest mathematics prize of her time, the Prix Bordin. She worked on a problem about the rings around the planet Saturn. When the Paris Academy of Sciences *announced* the winner, everyone was amazed that it was a woman. They gave Kovalevsky twice the usual prize money, because she had solved a problem that was very important to science.

In 1890, Sofia Kovalevsky became the first woman elected to the St. Petersburg Imperial *Academy* of Science. Unfortunately, her life and brilliant career ended early. In December 1890, she caught a cold. She got very sick, and she died on February 10, 1891, at the age of 41.

一位瑞典的大数学家帮助科瓦列夫斯基在瑞典找到一个数学教授的职位。由于她是除了在意大利之外欧洲唯一的一位女教授，她成了名人。1888年，科瓦列夫斯基参加了她那个时代数学的最高奖项——博尔丁奖的角逐。她致力于解决围绕土星的土星环问题。当巴黎科学院宣布该奖得主时，大家惊奇地发现获奖者竟是一位女性。她获得的奖金是正常奖金的两倍，因为她解决了科学上一个非常重要的问题。

1890年，索菲亚·科瓦列夫斯基成了圣彼得堡皇家科学院的第一名女院士。不幸的是，她的生活和辉煌的事业过早地结束了。1890年她患了感冒，病得很重，于1891年2月10日去世，享年41岁。

---

announce *v.* 宣布

academy *n.* 学院

Vincent Van Gogh

Today, a painting by Vincent Van Gogh sells for more than $80 million. But while he was alive, no one wanted to buy his work. Most people either *ignored* him or laughed at him.

Vincent van Gogh was born in 1853 in Groot-Zundert, Holland. His father was a church minister. He taught Vincent that it was important to help others. Van Gogh tried to be a *minister* too, but he was not successful. He tried many other

---

文森特·梵高

如今，文森特·梵高的一幅画能卖八千多万美元，但他活着时，谁也不想买他的作品。大多数人要么无视他，要么嘲笑他。

文森特·梵高1853年生于荷兰的赫罗特津德尔特。他父亲是牧师，曾教导文森特说，帮助他人是很重要的。梵高也想当一名牧师，但没有实

---

ignore *v.* 忽视

minister *n.* 牧师

jobs also. He worked as an art seller, a bookseller, and a teacher. He failed at each one. Unfortunately, van Gogh had mental problems and was often sad or angry. This made it difficult for him to succeed.

Van Gogh was very good at one thing—art. He taught himself to draw and paint. Van Gogh drew all the time. He drew on anything he could find—*menus*, books, and scraps of paper. In 1881, he began to study art, first in Brussels, then in Paris. His early paintings were about poor people in Holland. They were dark pictures and the people in them were sad. When he went to France, he started to paint with bright colors. He painted in an exciting way, and his paintings showed his strong feelings. He always painted the *ordinary* things in life—his bedroom, a chair, or some flowers. Often he went into the country to paint birds, flowers, and fields.

Van Gogh's paintings were very different from the paintings of other artists, and people didn't like them. Sometimes he left his

---

现愿望。他还尝试过许多别的工作，当过画店和书店店员，当过教师，每个工作都没有干成。不幸的是，梵高有精神病，常常悲伤或生气，这使他很难获得成功。

梵高非常擅长一件事——美术。他自学绘画。梵高不停地画，在他能找到的一切东西——菜单、书以及纸片上面画。1881年，他开始学习绘画艺术，先是在布鲁塞尔，然后去了巴黎。他的早期画作画的都是荷兰的穷人，画面暗淡，人物抑郁。他到了法国后，开始用明亮的颜色作画。他作画时情绪亢奋，画作表达了他的强烈情感。他总是画日常生活中的一些东西——他的卧室、椅子或花卉。他还常到乡下去画鸟类、花草和田野。

梵高的绘画与其他画家的绘画迥然不同，未能受人青睐。有时，在搬

---

menu *n.* 菜单　　　　　　　　　　ordinary *adj.* 普通的；平常的

paintings when he moved to a different place. When people found the paintings, they used them for firewood or to build things. He couldn't sell his work, so he didn't have much money. He often did not have food to eat because he used his money to buy paints and brushes. He also gave clothes and food to other poor people.

Van Gogh's mental problems made his life very difficult. He had a strange, *moody* personality. He was *stubborn* and liked to argue. Some people were afraid of him. Others laughed at him. Children threw things at him in the street and called him bad names. His brother Theo was his only real friend. Theo was an art seller. He believed that Vincent was a genius. Theo gave him money and encouraged him to keep working.

Van Gogh spent the last two years of his life in southern France. During this time, he created almost 200 paintings. In 1888, French artist Paul Gaugin went to live with van Gogh. One night they had

---

家当中他把画弄丢了。别人发现这些画时，只把它们当柴火或制作其他物品用。他的作品卖不出去，所以他没有钱。他常常没有饭吃，因为钱都花在买颜料和画笔上了。他还把衣服和食物送给别的穷人。

梵高的精神病使他的日子很艰难。他个性奇特、喜怒无常；他很固执而且喜欢争论。有些人惧怕他，有些人则嘲笑他。在街上，孩子们向他扔东西，还给他起难听的绰号。他的弟弟特奥是他唯一的、真正的朋友。特奥是画品销售商，他深信文森特是个天才。特奥周济哥哥并鼓励他继续画下去。

梵高生命中的最后两年是在法国南部度过的。这期间，他创作了近二百幅画。1888年，法国艺术家保罗·高更也和梵高住在一起。一天夜

---

moody *adj.* 喜怒无常的   stubborn *adj.* 固执的

a terrible argument. Van Gogh chased Gaugin down a street with a *razor*. Later van Gogh was very sorry. He went home and cut off a piece of his left ear. He lost so much blood that he almost died.

Van Gogh realized that he needed help. He went to a mental hospital. While he was there, he continued to paint. In fact, in the last 70 days of his life, he painted a picture every day. He painted one of his best works, *Starry Night*, while he was looking out from his bedroom window at the hospital. Van Gogh went in and out of mental hospitals for many months. Finally, on July 27, 1890, he shot himself. He died two days later. He was only 37 years old.

Theo was full of sorrow over his brother's death. He became sick and died only six months later. He was just 33 years old. Theo's *widow*, Johanna, worked hard to make van Gogh and his paintings well known. Less than 30 years after his death, van Gogh was called one of the greatest artists of all time.

里，他俩吵得很厉害。梵高拿着剃刀追赶高更，一直追到街上。事后，梵高很后悔，他回到家中，将自己的左耳割掉了一块。他失血过多，差一点死去。

梵高意识到他需要治疗了，来到一家精神病院。住院期间，他继续作画。实际上，在他生命的最后70天中，他每天都画一幅画。正是从病房的窗户向外观察而生灵感，他画出了最佳作品之一——《星夜》。好几个月里，梵高时进时出精神病院。最终，于1890年7月27日，梵高向自己开了枪。两天后他去世了，年仅37岁。

对于哥哥的死，特奥悲痛欲绝。他病倒了，6个月后也离开了人世，去世时才33岁。特奥的遗孀约翰娜竭尽全力使世人了解梵高和他的画作。梵高死后不到30年，人们便称他为世上最伟大的画家之一。

---

razor *n.* 刀片　　　　　　　　　　　　　　widow *n.* 寡妇

31

Maggle Walker

Maggie Walker was born in 1867 in Richmond, Virginia. Her mother was once a slave in a rich woman's house. When Maggie was very young, a thief killed her father. Her family was poor, so Maggie's mother started doing *laundry* in her home. Maggie had to help her. She washed clothes every day, but she continued to go to school. She was a very good student, especially in math.

After Maggie graduated from high school, she got a job as a teacher. In 1886, she married Armistead Walker. They had two sons and Maggie stayed home to care for them. She also volunteered to help a social *organization* called the Order of St. Luke. This

---

玛吉·瓦尔克

玛吉·瓦尔克1867年出生于弗吉尼亚州的里士满。她的母亲曾经在一富婆家当奴隶,玛吉小时父亲就被一盗贼杀害。由于家境贫穷,母亲开始在家做些洗衣的活计,玛吉也得做母亲的帮手。她每天洗衣,仍坚持去上学。她是个好学生,数学特别好。

玛吉高中毕业后找到一份当老师的工作。1886年她和阿米斯特德·瓦尔克结婚,婚后生有二子,玛吉留在家照看孩子。她还志愿帮助一个叫作"圣卢

---

laundry *n.* 洗衣   organization *n.* 组织

organization helped African Americans take care of the sick and bury the dead. Maggie Walker loved the work of the organization. The organization believed that African Americans should take care of each other.

Over the years, Maggie Walker had more and more responsibilities with the organization. In 1895, she suggested that St. Luke begin a program for young people. This *program* became very popular with schoolchildren. In 1899, Walker became Grand Secretary Treasurer of the St. Luke organization. However, because she was a woman, she received less than half the salary of the man who had the job before her.

The Order of St. Luke had a lot of *financial* difficulties when Walker

---

克安抚会"的社会组织做事。该组织帮助非洲裔的美国人照看病人和安葬死者。玛吉喜欢这个组织的工作,该组织认为非裔美国人应该相互帮助。

多年来,玛吉在该组织中担负着越来越多的职责。1895年经她提议,圣卢克为年轻人开办了一个服务项目,该项目在学童中深受欢迎。1899年她担任该组织的财务秘书长。因为她是女性,她的工资还不到她的男性前任的一半。

玛吉接管这项工作时,该组织正面临巨大的财政危机,许多账单尚未

---

program *n.* 项目

financial *adj.* 财政的

took over. It had a lot of unpaid bills and only $31.61 in the bank. But soon Maggie Walker changed all of that. Her idea was to get new members to join the organization. In just a few years, it grew from 3,400 members to 50,000 members. The organization bought a $100,000 office building and increased its staff to 55. Now Walker was ready for her next big step.

In 1903, Walker decided the organization needed its own bank. So she helped to *establish* the St. Luke Penny Savings Bank. Maggie Walker became its president—she was the first woman to be a bank president in the United States. The bank was very important for African Americans. It gave loans to families so they could buy their own homes. The bank also *encouraged* children to save money. They could save small amounts of money in a little box the bank gave them. Then they could open a savings account with only $1. But

---

支付，银行只存有31.61美元。玛吉很快改变了这一切。她的办法是吸收新会员加入该组织。仅仅几年内，该组织从3400人增加到50,000人。该组织购置了价值100,000美元的办公大楼，工作人员增加到55人。那时玛吉已经为她迈开更大的下一步做好了准备。

1903年，玛吉决定该组织要创办自己的银行，因此，她协助筹建了圣卢克小额储蓄银行。玛吉成了该行行长，同时也是美国第一位女银行行长。该银行对非裔美国人非常重要，可以为不少家庭提供贷款购房。银行还鼓励儿童存钱，孩子们可以把小额零钱存放在银行发给他们的小盒子里。尔后孩子们可以在银行开一个哪怕只有一美元的存折。不过，玛吉

---

establish *v.* 建立   encourage *v.* 鼓励

Walker's hard work and generosity also helped white people. Other banks wouldn't give the city schools more money. St. Luke gave them a loan and saved the school system. The bank still exists today under the name Consolidated Bank and Trust Company.

Walker was not only a businesswoman. She always found time to help her *community*. She published a newspaper called the St. Luke Herald, raised money for a girls' school, started a visiting nurse service for the poor and sick, and helped to build a hospital. In 1907, Walker fell and was never able to walk again. She was in a wheelchair for the rest of her life. But she continued her work at the newspaper and the bank for almost 30 more years.

In 1915, something terrible happened in the Walker house. Maggie's son shot her husband, Armistead, by mistake because he thought Armistead was a thief. There was a trial, and Walker supported her son all the time. Luckily, he did not go to *prison*.

的勤奋工作和慷慨大度也帮助了白人。其他银行不会给市立学校贷更多的钱，而圣卢克却给学校贷款，挽救了学校。银行的这种制度一直延续到今天，其名称为统一银行和信托公司。

玛吉不仅是一位女实业家，还经常挤时间帮助社区工作。她出版了一份圣卢克先驱报，为一女子学校筹措款项，为穷困病人开设上门护理服务，并协助创办了一家医院。1907年玛吉摔倒在地，从此再也不能走路了，她在轮椅上度过了余生。但是，她仍为报纸和银行工作了近三十年。

1915年，玛吉家中大祸降临，她的儿子开枪打死了父亲阿米斯特德。其实，这是一场误会，儿子误认为父亲是个贼。审讯中，玛吉始终支持儿子。幸好，儿子没有被送进监狱。

---

community *n.* 社区   prison *n.* 监狱

In 1932, Maggie Walker retired from the bank. She died two years later. Her funeral was one of the largest in the history of Richmond. The city named a high school, a theater, and a street after her. The Walkers' home is now a national *historic site*.

1932年，玛吉·瓦尔克从银行退休，两年后去世。她的葬礼是里士满历史上最隆重的葬礼之一。该市以她的名字命名了一所中学、一座剧院和一条街道。瓦尔克的故居现为国家历史圣地。

historic *adj.* 历史上著名的　　　　　　　　　　site *n.* 地点；场所

32

Helena Rubinstein

In 1950, Helena Rubinstein was one of the richest women in the world. She started with nothing. She had no money, no education, and no one to help her. All she had were 12 *jars* of face cream and a lot of energy and ambition. She turned these into a multimillion-dollar *cosmetics* empire.

Helena Rubinstein was born in 1870 in Krakow, Poland. She was the oldest of eight girls. Helena's mother thought that beauty was very important. She used a special skin cream that a Hungarian chemist made for her. Helena's mother made all of her daughters use it too.

海伦娜·鲁宾施泰因

1950年，海伦娜·鲁宾施泰因成为世界上最富有的女人之一。她白手起家，身无分文，没有受过教育，无人相助。她的全部家当就是12瓶面霜以及充沛的精力和勃勃雄心。她把这些转变成了价值数百万美元的化妆品王国。

海伦娜·鲁宾施泰因1870年出生在波兰的克拉科夫，是家中8个女孩中的长女。她母亲认为仪容漂亮非常重要，她使用一位匈牙利化学家专门为她研制的一种护肤霜，让所有的女儿也用这种护肤霜。

jar n. 广口瓶   cosmetic *n.* 化妆品

Helena's father wanted her to be a doctor. But she hated medicine and left school. Her father was very angry. Then he wanted her to get married, but she refused. In 1902, she went to Melbourne, Australia, to live with a cousin and an uncle. She took only her clothes and 12 jars of the face cream.

HR HELENA RUBINSTEIN

Helena didn't speak English. She had no money and no plans. After she arrived, everyone noticed her beautiful skin. In Australia the hot, dry weather is very bad for the *skin*. When she told some of the women about the *face cream*, they all wanted some. Helena sold

---

海伦娜的父亲想让她成为一名医生，而她讨厌医学并放弃了学业。父亲为此非常生气，便让她结婚，又被她一口拒绝。1902年她去了澳大利亚的墨尔本，和叔叔、堂兄生活在一起。她仅带了几件随身穿的衣服和12瓶面霜。

海伦娜不会说英语，没有钱，也没有明确的计划。她抵达那里后，人们注意到她的美丽肌肤。澳大利亚炎热干燥的气候对皮肤非常有害，当她和一些妇女谈起面霜的事时，这些妇女都想买来试试。海伦娜卖了一些给她们后又续订了很多。

---

skin *n.* 皮肤　　　　　　　　　　　　　　　　　face cream 面霜

them her cream and then ordered more.

Helena borrowed $1,500 and opened a shop to sell the cream. She worked 18 hours a day, seven days a week. She lived simply and saved all of her profits. She also learned how to make different kinds of creams and showed women how to take care of their skin. It was the first shop of this kind in the world.

In less than two years, Rubinstein had paid back her *loan* and saved $50,000. She made more and more money every year. All this time, she thought only of work and success. A newspaper *reporter* named Edward Titus was in love with her. But she was not interested in him. She left Australia and went to Europe to learn more about the science of beauty.

海伦娜借了1500美元开了个面霜商店。她每周工作7天，每天工作18小时。她生活简朴，积蓄了所有盈利。她还学习怎样制作不同种类的霜膏，并指导妇女们如何护肤。这种商店是当时世界上的首创。

不到两年，她便还清了借债并积蓄了50,000美元，而且每年赚的钱越来越多。这段时间她满脑子想的是工作和成功。一位叫作爱德华·泰特斯的报纸记者爱上了她，但她对这个人不感兴趣。她离开澳大利亚前往欧洲学习更多的美容科学知识。

---

loan *n.* 贷款

reporter *n.* 记者

In 1908, Helena decided to open a shop in London. Everyone told her she was crazy because English women didn't use beauty products. But she didn't listen. Her shop was a big success. Meanwhile, Titus went to London and convinced her to marry him. In 1909, they had a son. Two years later, she moved her family to Paris and opened another shop. In 1912, they had another son.

Helena Rubinstein wasn't a very good wife or mother. Her work was the most important thing to her, and she dreamed only of *expanding* her business. She wanted everyone to be like her, especially the people who worked for her. She paid them very little money and they worked very hard. But Helena was never *satisfied*. She always thought they should do more.

1908年海伦娜决定在伦敦开一家美容店。大家都说她发疯了，因为英国女人不使用美容品。但她并不理会这些言论。她的店铺生意兴隆，大获成功。此时，泰特斯也赶到伦敦说服她与自己成婚。1909年，他们喜得一子。两年后，他们举家迁居巴黎，开了另一家分店。1912年，他们又得一子。

海伦娜·鲁宾施泰因不是贤妻良母，对她来说，最重要的莫过于工作，她唯一的梦想是不断扩大她的事业。她要求人人都像她那样敬业，特别是为她干活的那些人。她只付给下属低薪酬，却要他们卖命地去干活。而即使这样，海伦娜也从未满意过，她总是认为他们应该干得更多。

---

expand *v.* 扩张；扩大　　　　　　　satisfied *adj.* 感到满意的

In 1915, Rubinstein moved her family to the United States. She wanted to open a shop in New York City. Again, people told her it was foolish. At that time, respectable American women didn't wear lipstick or makeup. Again, Rubinstein knew better. By 1917, she had seven shops in the United States and one in Canada. In addition, thousands of shops and department stores sold her products. She was a great success. People called her "the beauty *queen*." Strangely, she never followed her own beauty advice because she never had time!

Rubinstein was a *workaholic*. She never stopped working, and she ignored her family. Her husband once told her, "Nothing will ever change you, Helena. Your business is your life." They divorced in 1930.

1915年，鲁宾施泰因举家迁居美国，她想在纽约市再开一家分店。人们再一次告诫她，说这是愚蠢的。那时，美国的贵妇们从不使用唇膏和化妆品。海伦娜又一次显示了她的先见之明，到1917年，她在美国已开设了7家分店，在加拿大还开设了一家分店。另外，数千家商店和百货公司在销售她的产品。她获得了巨大的成功，人们称她为"美容皇后"。奇怪的是她从不遵循自己常向他人所做的有关美容的忠告，因为她根本就挤不出时间。

鲁宾施泰因是个工作狂。她不停地工作，忽略了对家庭的照料。一次她丈夫对她说："海伦娜，看来任何事情也不能改变你，你的生意就是你的生命。"1930年，他们离异了。

---

queen *n.* 皇后；王后　　　　　　　　workaholic *n.* 工作狂

Helena Rubinstein was a *ruthless* businesswoman. Her money gave her great power. She used it to buy possessions and people. In 1938, she married *Prince* Gourielli. He was 20 years younger than she was, and he had no money or power. But he was a prince and she liked that very much. When he died in 1956, she didn't even return from her vacation for his funeral. "He's dead," she said. "Why waste the money?"

Rubinstein was very strange about money. She spent thousands of dollars on travel, jewelry, and art. But she also ate lunch at her desk because it was cheaper than going out. She argued with taxi drivers about how much to pay them. She used the stairs instead of the elevator to save electricity. And she never retired. Rubinstein continued working until she died at the age of 94.

海伦娜·鲁宾施泰因是个无情的女实业家。金钱赋予她巨大的权力，她用此索购财宝甚至人身。1938年她和小她20岁的古里力王子结婚。古里力既无钱又无权，但其王子的身份令她欢喜有加。所以，1956年王子去世时，鲁宾施泰因甚至照常度假，没有参加丈夫的葬礼。"他死了，"鲁宾施泰因说道，"何必浪费钱？"

鲁宾施泰因在花钱方面非常怪诞。她把成千上万的美元花在旅游、购买珠宝和艺术品上，却总是在办公桌上用午餐，因为这样比到外面吃便宜。她常为付费多少和出租车司机争吵。为了节省电，她宁愿走楼梯而不乘电梯。她一直工作到去世也没有退休，享年94岁。

---

ruthless *adj.* 无情的

prince *n.* 王子

33

Julia Morgan

In 1919, a very rich American named William Randolph Hearst wanted to build a new house. Most rich people lived in mansions, but Hearst wanted something bigger and more elegant. He wanted a castle. He hired architect Julia Morgan to design it for him. Hearst Castle in San Simeon, California is now one of the most famous buildings in the world. This *extravagant* house has 58 bedrooms, 61 bathrooms, a theater, and a zoo! Morgan worked on it for more than 20 years. Hearst Castle is her most famous work, but she also built more than 800 other buildings. Her great talent and success helped other women to become *architects*.

朱莉娅·摩根

1919年，一位叫作威廉·兰道夫·赫斯特的美国富豪想建一处新寓所。那时，大多数富豪都住在大楼里，但赫斯特想拥有更为宏伟、优雅的建筑。他要把大厦建成一座城堡。他雇了建筑师朱莉娅·摩根为他设计。赫斯特城堡位于加利福尼亚的圣西米恩，是当今世界闻名的建筑之一。这座奢华的殿堂有58间卧室，61间浴室，一座剧院，甚至还有一个动物园！摩根为此耗时二十余年。赫斯特城堡是她的杰作，此外，她还建过八百多座楼宇。她的天才和成就激励了其他女性走上建筑师岗位。

architect *n.* 建筑师；设计师　　　　　extravagant *adj.* 奢侈的；浪费的

Julia Morgan was born in 1872 to a wealthy family in San Francisco, California. She had one sister and three brothers. Julia was a small, weak child, but her mother encouraged her to work hard. She studied hard and did very well in school. After she finished high school, Julia went to the University

of California at Berkeley. In those days, few women went to college. In fact, Julia was often the only woman in her math and science classes. In 1894, she became the first woman to graduate from the university with a *degree* in civil *engineering*.

One of Julia's teachers was an architect named Bernard Maybeck. After graduation, Julia went to work as his assistant. He

---

朱莉娅·摩根1872年生于加利福尼亚州旧金山的一个富有家庭，她有一个姐姐和三个哥哥。朱莉娅是个弱小的女孩，但她母亲鼓励她勤奋上进。她努力学习，成绩优秀。中学毕业后，朱莉娅进了加州大学伯克利分校。那时，几乎没有女子能进大学。事实上，在数学和科技课上朱莉娅经常是唯一的女生。1894年，朱莉娅成了从这所大学毕业并取得土木工程学学位的第一位女生。

朱莉娅的一位老师叫作伯纳德·梅贝克，是位建筑师。毕业后，她当了这位老师的助手。老师鼓励她申请去巴黎美术学院学习，该学院是当时世界

---

degree *n.* 学位　　　　　　　　　　engineering *n.* 工程；工程学

encouraged her to apply to the Éole des Beaux-Arts in Paris. The Éole was the most famous art school in the world at that time. In 1896, Julia left for Paris to study for the *entrance* exams.

In Paris, Julia Morgan worked for a French architect for two years. She practiced drawing and designing. She also learned to speak and write in French. Morgan failed the entrance exams two times but she was not *discouraged*. Most students failed them at least twice. On her third try, she passed. She was the first woman to attend the Éole des Beaux-Arts, but she was not allowed to sit with her classmates. She had to sit behind a screen in all her classes because she was a woman. In 1902, Morgan became the first woman to graduate from the Éole's department of architecture.

Morgan returned to California and became the first woman to receive an architect's license. In 1904, she opened her own architectural office. Morgan was talented and soon had a lot of

---

上最有名的艺术学院。1896年，朱莉娅赴法国巴黎学习，准备入学考试。

在巴黎，朱莉娅·摩根为一位法国建筑师工作了两年。她练习绘图和设计，还学习用法语交谈和写作。两次入学考试都失败了，但她不气馁，大多数学生也至少失败两次。朱莉娅第三次考试通过了，她是到巴黎美术学院就读的第一个女生，但她却不能和同班同学坐在一起，她上所有的课都必须坐在一道屏幕的后面，只因她是女生。1902年，她成为巴黎美术学院建筑系毕业的第一位女生。

朱莉娅回到加利福尼亚，成了第一个获得建筑师证书的女性。1904年，她开设了自己的建筑事务所。她非常能干，很快就接到了许多工程。这期间，最重要的工程是重建位于旧金山的费尔蒙特酒店，该酒店曾在

---

entrance *n.* 入学　　　　　　　　　discourage *v.* 使泄气

work. Her most important project during this time was rebuilding the Fairmont Hotel in San Francisco. An earthquake in 1906 had destroyed it. After Morgan completed the Fairmont, she had so much work that she hired assistants to help her. She tried to *hire* women whenever possible. She also gave money to several schools to help female architecture students.

In 1915, William Randolph Hearst hired Morgan to design a Los Angeles office building. Four years later, he asked her to build the castle. Hearst was very demanding. He wrote Morgan hundreds of letters full of instructions, and he often changed his mind. Sometimes he told her to build something, then he told her to take it down and rebuild it in another place. In the end, he sometimes asked her to rebuild it a third time in its original place! Morgan's work was *meticulous*. She paid careful attention to Hearst's requests and wasn't afraid of hard work. She wore pants under her skirt and

---

1906年的一次地震中被毁。她完成了费尔蒙特酒店的重建工程后，接到的工程项目太多，不得不雇一名助手帮忙。只要有可能，她尽量雇用女性，她还出钱资助一些学校建筑专业的女生。

1915年，威廉·兰道夫·赫斯特雇请朱莉娅为他设计一座洛杉矶写字楼。四年后，他请朱莉娅建设那座城堡。赫斯特非常苛求。他写给朱莉娅数百封满纸要求及说明的信，而且经常改变主意。有时，他让朱莉娅建造某个建筑，尔后又让她推倒，在另一个地方重建。最后，又让她推倒，在原先的地方建造第三次。朱莉娅在工作中非常小心谨慎，她对赫斯特的要求一丝不苟，不畏艰苦。她会在裙下套上工作裤，爬上梯子检查工作，事

---

hire *v.* 雇用   meticulous *adj.* 小心的

climbed ladders to check the work herself. For more than 20 years she traveled 200 miles from San Francisco to San Simeon three weekends a month. For all of her work over so many years, Morgan received only $70,000.

Morgan never married. She was always busy with her work, so she didn't have time for other interests or much of a social life. Her only social life was to visit her mother and her married sister. Morgan had surgery that left her face *crooked* and also affected the way she spoke and moved. But she still continued to design schools, churches, public buildings and private homes.

In 1946, at age 74, Julia Morgan closed her office and traveled for the rest of her life. She died in 1957 at the age of 85. Her buildings still *influence* architects today.

必躬亲。二十多年中,她每个月有3个周末穿梭于相距200英里的旧金山和圣西米恩之间。朱莉娅这么多年的全部工作报酬仅得到了70,000美元。

朱莉娅一生未婚。他总是忙于工作,无暇顾及其他兴趣和社交生活。她唯一的社交生活就是看望她的母亲和已婚的姐姐。朱莉娅做过外科手术,致使她的脸有些扭曲变形,说话和动作也受到影响,但她仍然不停地为学校、教堂、公共建筑和私人住宅做设计。

1946年,朱莉亚74岁时关闭了她的建筑事务所,开始周游各地,以享余生。朱莉亚·摩根于1957年去世,享年85岁。她的建筑风格仍然影响着当今的建筑师。

---

crook *v.* 使弯曲   influence *v.* 影响

34

Princess Ka'iulani

On October 16, 1875, a child was born in Hawaii. Her name was Victoria Ka'iulani. Ka'iulani was a princess because her uncle, King Kalakaua, did not have children. So the people of Hawaii were very happy when Ka'iulani was born. Ka'iulani's childhood was like a fairy tale. The little princess played with giant *turtles* and *fed* beautiful birds

卡伊乌拉妮公主

1875年10月16日，一个婴儿诞生在夏威夷，她叫维多利亚·卡伊乌拉妮。因为她的叔叔——国王卡拉卡瓦没有子女，所以，卡伊乌拉妮就成了公主。夏威夷的百姓得知卡伊乌拉妮降生，都非常高兴。卡伊乌拉妮的童年就像童话一般，小公主和巨龟一起嬉戏，在岛上的家里喂养美丽的小鸟。她还骑着白马驰骋，在海边冲浪、戏水。她是个甜美快乐的孩子，人人都喜欢她。

turtle *n.* 龟

feed *v.* 喂养

on her island home. She rode a white horse and went *surfing* and swimming. She was a sweet, happy child, and everyone loved her.

Ka'iulani's fairy tale ended when she was only 11 years old. Her mother, Princess Likelike, suddenly became very ill. The day Likelike died, she told her daughter, "You will go far away from your land and your people. You will never marry and you will never be queen of Hawaii."

Ka'iulani was very sad after her mother's death. She was then second in line to be queen after her aunt, Liliuokalani. Ka'iulani needed to prepare to be queen. She had to learn about the world around her. When she was 14 years old, she went to England to study. Ka'iulani was afraid to leave her home, but she had to. It was her *royal* duty. Her father sailed with her to San Francisco. Then she took a train to New York and another ship across the Atlantic Ocean. It was a long and difficult journey.

卡伊乌拉妮11岁时，她童话般的生活便宣告结束了，她母亲莱克莱克公主突然病倒。母亲去世那天嘱咐她说："你要远走高飞，离开你的国土和人民。你永远不要结婚，永远也不要当夏威夷的女王。"

母亲去世后，卡伊乌拉妮非常悲伤。她排在她姑姑里留奥卡莱妮之后，成了第二位有可能当女王的人。她需要作当女王的准备，也必须学习以了解周围的世界。卡伊乌拉妮14岁时前往英国学习。她害怕离开家乡，但又不得不走，这是她的皇家职责。父亲乘船送她到旧金山，然后她乘火车到纽约，又乘另一艘船越过大西洋。这真是一次长途跋涉。

---

surf *v.* 冲浪   royal *adj.* 皇家的

Ka'iulani went to a private girls' school in England. She made friends easily and loved to study. She was very happy there, but she missed Hawaii. She wrote cheerful letters to her family and friends. But the letters from home gave her more and more bad news.

For many years, other countries wanted to control the Hawaiian Islands. Hawaii was a perfect place for *ports* and *military* bases. When Ka'iulani left Hawaii, her country was already in danger. A group of American businessmen were telling King Kalakaua what to do. Many of them were the sons of religious missionaries. These missionaries had gone to the islands in the 1800s to teach Hawaiians about Christianity. They wanted the Hawaiians to learn a new religion, culture, language, and government. Over the years their families had become rich and powerful. They often treated the Hawaiians badly. Eventually, these men controlled the government and all the important businesses. In 1891, they forced King Kalakaua to give

---

卡伊乌拉妮在英国一所私人女子学校就读。她平易近人、善于交友，也喜欢学习。在那里她过得很愉快，只是有些思念夏威夷。她给家里和朋友写了很多令人高兴的信，可是家中的来信总是带给她愈来愈多的坏消息。

多年来，别的国家一直觊觎夏威夷岛国，因为它是个十分理想的港口和军事基地。当卡伊乌拉妮离开夏威夷时，她的国家已处于危难之中。一帮美国商人要卡拉卡瓦国王按他们的旨意行事。这些商人中的许多人是传教士的后裔，他们早在19世纪初就来到岛上向夏威夷人传授基督教。他们要夏威夷人学习新的宗教、文化、语言和政体。若干年后，他们的家族变得富有且有权势。他们对待夏威夷人总是很坏。最后，这些人控制了政府和一切重要的经济事务。1891他们逼迫卡拉卡瓦国王放弃一些权力，要

---

port *n.* 港口

military *adj.* 军事的

up some of his powers. They wanted Hawaii to be under American control. They wanted to *annex* Hawaii to the United States.

King Kalakaua tried to stop the Americans. But he died suddenly and his sister, Liliuokalani, became queen. She was stronger than her brother, and she did not listen to the Americans. They could not control her, so they forced her to give up her power. Then they *established* their own government.

Ka'iulani was devastated when she heard this news. She wanted to help her people, but she didn't know what to do. She decided to talk to the President of the United States, Grover Cleveland. Ka'iulani was only 17 years old. She was afraid, but she had to try to save her country.

Ka'iulani went to the United States and met the President. While she was there, she made many speeches. She wanted the American people to help Hawaii. People respected her for her courage and

---

夏威夷受控于美国，他们要让夏威夷沦为美国的附庸。

　　卡拉卡瓦国王竭力抵制美国人，但他突然驾崩。他的妹妹里留奥卡莱妮成了女王。她比她哥哥强硬，不听从美国人。美国人控制不了她，就迫使她放弃权力。尔后他们竟私自建立了自己的政府。

　　卡伊乌拉妮闻讯后，气得发昏。她想帮助她的人民，但不知道该怎么办。于是她决定去找美国总统格罗弗·克利夫兰理论此事。卡伊乌拉妮当时年仅17岁，尽管有些胆怯，但她必须设法拯救她的国家。

　　卡伊乌拉妮前往美国见到了总统。她在那里时作了许多演讲，希望美国人民能帮助夏威夷。人们十分敬佩她的勇气和尊严。克利夫兰总统请求

---

annex *v.* 附加　　　　　　　　establish *v.* 建立

dignity. President Cleveland asked Congress to allow Liliuokalani to be queen again. But the Americans in Hawaii refused to give up their new government. In 1897, Congress voted to annex Hawaii. The Hawaiians were angry and sad, but they couldn't do anything. They were now a *minority* in their own country because so many other people had moved there.

Ka'iulani went home to be with her people. She tried to bring them peace and happiness, but it was *impossible*. At age 23, Ka'iulani became very ill. She was full of despair and was too weak to fight her illness. On March 6, 1899, Ka'iulani died. As her mother told her, she traveled far, she never married, and she never became queen of Hawaii.

国会应允里留奥卡莱妮再次担任女王，但夏威夷的美国人拒绝放弃他们的新政府。1897年美国国会投票赞成吞并夏威夷。夏威夷人民既愤怒又伤心，却无能为力。现在他们成了自己国家中的少数民族，因为相当多的其他地域的人移居到了那里。

卡伊乌拉妮回到家乡同她的人民在一起，她尽其全力要带给人们和平与幸福。然而，这是不可能的。23岁时，她身患重病，满腹绝望。此时，她的身体虚弱之极，已无力与病魔抗争，于1899年3月6日病故。正如她母亲叮嘱她的那样，她曾远走他乡，从未婚嫁，也没有去当夏威夷的女王。

---

minority *n.* 少数 　　　　　　　　　　　impossible *adj.* 不可能的

Isadora Duncan

Isadora Duncan always wanted to be different. She loved to dance, but she didn't like *traditional* dances. She refused to learn classical ballet. Instead, Isadora listened to the music and moved *naturally*. She walked, jumped, or just stood still and moved from side to

Isadora Duncan

伊莎多拉·邓肯

伊莎多拉·邓肯总想标新立异，与众不同。她酷爱跳舞，但不喜欢传统的舞蹈方式。她不屑于去学经典芭蕾舞，而喜欢随着音乐自然起舞。她的舞姿，包括行进、跳跃或原地不动而双侧轮流做动作，都很新颖，以前，从来没有人像她那样跳舞。她是现代舞的创始人。

---

traditional *adj.* 传统的   naturally *adv.* 自然地

side. No one had ever danced like that before. She was the *creator* of modern dance.

Isadora Duncan was born in 1878 in San Francisco, California. She was the youngest of four children. Her parents got divorced soon after Isadora was born. Isadora's mother, Dora, always told her children that marriage was terrible. Isadora believed her and promised never to marry. Dora was a music teacher. She earned very little money, so the family was poor. They often couldn't pay the rent, so they moved from place to place. Dora believed that children should be free, so Isadora grew up with few rules. Dora also *encouraged* Isadora to dance and to love the arts.

At age 6, Isadora began to teach other children to dance. By age 10, she was so successful that she decided to quit school. She said school was a waste of time. Isadora had little formal education, but she taught herself a lot. She read books by all the great writers and

伊莎多拉·邓肯1878年生于加利福尼亚州的旧金山，是家里4个孩子中最小的一个。她出生不久父母就离异了。母亲多拉总是告诫孩子们结婚是很糟糕的事，伊莎多拉相信母亲的话，并答应永不嫁人。多拉是位音乐老师，挣钱很少，家境贫寒。她们因交不起房租，经常得把家从一地搬到另一地。多拉认为孩子们应当享有自由，因此，伊莎多拉的成长过程中很少受到约束。母亲还鼓励她跳舞，热爱艺术。

伊莎多拉6岁就能教其他孩子跳舞，10岁时她就跳得很出色了，便决定退学。她说上学纯属浪费时间。她接受正规教育很少，但她自学了很多知识，她阅读所有大作家的作品并学习艺术。

creator *n.* 创造人　　　　　　　　　　encourage *v.* 鼓励

studied the arts.

At age 16, Isadora tried to become a professional dancer. She couldn't find a job because nobody liked her *style* of dancing. She went from city to city, year after year. Everyone turned her away, but she tried very hard. When she was 18 years old, she got a small part in a play in New York City. She stayed there for a while, then she decided she wanted to go to London. Isadora didn't have much money, so some of her friends gave her money. Life in London was very difficult at first. But after a while, people noticed her. They liked her *unique* way of dancing. Rich people asked her to dance at their parties. As the years went by, Duncan became famous and danced in all the great cities of Europe. Her lifestyle became famous too. She shocked everyone. She had two children by two different men from two different countries. She didn't marry either of them.

Isadora Duncan adored her children. Unfortunately, in 1913

伊莎多拉16岁时就想当一名专业舞蹈家，但她找不到工作，因为没有人喜欢她的舞蹈风格。一年又一年，她从一个城市转到另一个城市，仍然没有人聘请她，但她非常执着。18岁时她在纽约市上演的一个剧中扮演一小角色。她在那儿待了一小段时间，尔后决定去伦敦。伊莎多拉没有多少钱，她的朋友们给了一些资助。开始，在伦敦的生活很艰辛，过了一段时间，人们开始留意她，喜欢她独特的舞蹈风格。富人们请她到家中为聚会跳舞助兴。时来运转，邓肯名声大噪，她在欧洲各大城市跳舞。她的生活方式也为世人所瞩目，而且常令人惊诧。她和两个不同国籍的男人生下两个孩子，但她和这两个男人都没有结婚。

伊莎多拉·邓肯很喜欢她的两个孩子。不幸的是，1913年大祸降临。

---

style *n.* 风格　　　　　　　　　　　　　　　unique *adj.* 独特的

something horrible happened. Her children and their nurse were riding in a car in Paris. The car went out of control and rolled into the Seine River. All three of them drowned. Duncan was devastated. Her pain never went away.

Duncan opened several dance schools around Europe. All of them failed. She was a great dancer and millions of people *admired* her. But she wasn't a good businesswoman. She was only interested in her art. Sometimes she refused work because she didn't want to dance just for money. She decided things quickly and emotionally, so she made many bad *decisions*. Once, a group of Russians offered to open a school for her in Moscow, so she sold everything and went to Russia. When she got there, they changed their minds.

At age 44, Duncan broke her promise to her mother and got married. Her husband was Russian poet Sergei Yesenin, and he was 17 years younger than she was. The marriage was a terrible mistake.

两个孩子及其保姆驱车行驶在巴黎，汽车失去控制，冲入塞纳河，三人均溺水身亡。邓肯的精神崩溃了，这次灾难带来的痛苦始终萦绕在心头。

邓肯在欧洲开办了好几所舞蹈学校，不过均告失败。她是个伟大的舞蹈家，数以百万计的人钦慕她。但她不善从商，她只是对艺术感兴趣。有时她拒绝工作，因为她不想只为钱而跳舞。她处事果断却易感情用事。因此，她作了许多错误决定。一次一帮俄国人说要在莫斯科为她开办学校。为此，她变卖了一切，赶赴俄国。可是当她抵达那里时，那些俄国人却改变了主意。

邓肯44岁时，她违背了对母亲的承诺，结婚了。她的丈夫是俄国诗人谢尔盖·叶谢宁，比她小17岁。这是一桩十分错误的婚姻。叶谢宁神经

---

admire *v.* 钦慕　　　　　　　　　　　　　　　decision *n.* 决定

Yesenin had *mental* problems and a very bad *temper*. He threw chairs through windows and broke furniture and doors. Almost every day, he threatened to kill Duncan. During this time the couple was traveling a lot because Duncan was performing throughout Europe. When they got to Paris, Yesenin took all their money and went back to Russia. A year later, he committed suicide.

In 1927, Isadora Duncan moved to Nice, France. She was almost 50 years old and had very little money. But she never lost her energy and her love for life. One day she asked a car salesman for a ride in a sports car. She was dressed in a loose dress with a long scarf. She got into the car, waved to her friends, and said, "Good-bye, my friends, I am going to my glory." When the car started, her six-foot-long scarf got caught in the back wheel. The scarf tightened and broke her neck. Isadora Duncan died instantly.

有毛病，脾气极坏。他时常把椅子摔出窗外，砸坏家具和房门，几乎每天都威胁要杀死邓肯。这期间，他们夫妇周游了许多地方，因为邓肯四处表演，遍及欧洲。他们抵达巴黎时，叶谢宁卷走了所有的钱财，回到俄国，一年后自尽身亡。

1927年邓肯移居法国尼斯。那时她已年近半百，口袋里的钱寥寥无几，可她从未失去活力和对生活的热爱。一天，她请一位汽车推销员用一辆跑车带她兜风。此时，她身着宽松时装，并围了一条长围巾。她坐进车内，向朋友挥手道："再见，朋友们，我要走向辉煌。"跑车一启动，她的6英尺长的围巾缠到了后车轮上，围巾死死地勒断了她的脖子，伊莎多拉·邓肯当场丧命。

---

mental *adj.* 精神的　　　　　　　　　　　　　temper *n.* 脾气

Diego Rivera

Diego Rivera was born in 1886 in Guanajuato, Mexico. As a child, he was very intelligent and *curious* about everything. He grew up to be a strong and free-thinking man.

Diego graduated from art school at the head of his class. He left Mexico in 1907 and spent

---

迭戈·里韦拉

迭戈·里韦拉1886生于墨西哥的瓜纳华托州。他天资聪颖，小时候是个对什么都好奇的孩子，慢慢地成长为一个体魄健壮又善于自由想象的人。

迭戈毕业于美术学校，他的成绩在班上名列前茅。1907年他离开墨

---

curious *adj.* 好奇的

many of the next 14 years in Europe. During this time, he continued to study art. The paintings of European artists, such as Spanish painter Pablo Picasso, had a great *influence* on his work. Rivera was also very interested in *politics*. When he returned to Mexico in 1921, he wanted his art to be a part of the history of his country.

Mexico was not a democratic country at that time. But Rivera wanted Mexico to belong to all the people. He also believed that an artist's role was to fight for equality. Rivera thought his duty was to teach ordinary people with pictures. He wanted everyone to see his work, so he decided to paint murals. Murals are large pictures painted on the walls of buildings. His murals showed Mexican history, traditions, and culture.

The government gave Rivera permission to paint a mural on

西哥，在后来的14年中大部分时间在欧洲度过。这段时间里，他继续学习美术，欧洲艺术家如毕加索等的绘画对他的作品有很大影响。他对政治也十分关心。1921年回到墨西哥后，他希望他的艺术能成为他们国家历史的一部分。

那时，墨西哥还不是一个民主国家，但里韦拉希望他的国家属于全体人民。他还相信一个艺术家要在为人民争取平等权利中发挥作用。他认为他的责任是要以绘画教育普通百姓。他希望大家都看到他的作品，因此，他决定画壁画。壁画是将巨大的画面画在建筑物的墙上。他的壁画着力展现墨西哥的历史、传统和文化。

政府应允他在一所公立学校的建筑物上画壁画。这是他的第一幅重要

---

influence *n.* 影响　　　　　　　　　　　　politics *n.* 政治

a public school building. It was his first important mural, and it was very popular. Soon other painters in Mexico started painting murals too, and Mexico became the world center for mural painting. Altogether, Rivera painted more than two and a half miles of *murals* in his life. One painting had 124 parts. It showed Mexico's history. Rivera worked on this painting for more than four years. He did all the work himself and often worked 15 hours a day.

Rivera lived in the United States from 1930 to 1934. He painted public buildings in Detroit and San Francisco. But his mural in New York City caused trouble. Rivera was a *communist*, and he put the communist leader of Russia, Vladimir Lenin, in the mural. Many Americans were very angry about this. They destroyed the mural, and Rivera left the United States.

的壁画，非常受欢迎。不久，墨西哥的其他画家也开始画壁画，墨西哥成了世界壁画中心。里韦拉一生中画的壁画加起来总共有2.5英里长。有一幅壁画由124部分组成，它展示了墨西哥的历史。他为这件作品耗时四年多，绘制工作全部由自己动手，经常每天工作15个小时。

1930年至1934年里韦拉住在美国。他在底特律和旧金山的公共建筑物上绘画，他的壁画在纽约市却惹了麻烦。里韦拉是个共产主义者，他在壁画中画上了俄国共产党领袖列宁的像。许多美国人对此很愤怒，他们捣毁了壁画。里韦拉离开了美国。

---

mural *n.* 壁画　　　　　　　　　　　　　communist *n.* 共产主义者

Rivera was a very big man. He was over six feet tall and weighed over 300 pounds. He was also a great showman. People paid money just to watch him paint. When he painted, he told stories. Usually they were stories he made up about himself. People always wanted to hear more of his stories. Rivera had strong *opinions* about politics and religion, but people still admired him. He had many friends—especially women. He was married many times.

In 1928, Rivera married for the third time. He married artist Frida Kahlo. She was one of Mexico's greatest painters. Some people said she painted better than he did. Rivera always said Kahlo was the best *painter*, and Kahlo always said Rivera was the best. They loved

---

里韦拉是个体格魁梧的人，身高六英尺多，体重三百多磅。他也是一个善于表现自己的人。人们付钱只是为了观看他画画。他会一边作画，一边讲故事。一般都是讲他自己编排的故事，人们渴望听到他更多的故事。他的政治和宗教观点很激进，但人们仍然钦慕他。他有很多朋友，尤其是女性朋友。他曾多次结婚。

1928年里韦拉第三次结婚，娶了美术家弗里达·卡洛，她是墨西哥的大画家之一。有人认为她画得比里韦拉好。里韦拉总是说，卡洛是最好的画家，而卡洛则说里韦拉是最好的画家。他们彼此相爱，可婚姻生活中

---

opinion *n.* 观点　　　　　　　　　　　　　　painter *n.* 画家

each other, but their marriage was *stormy*. They had many fights and *separations*. They even divorced and remarried. Newspapers always wrote about "Frida and Diego." They lived in Mexico City in two separate houses with a bridge between them. Rivera's house was pink and Kahlo's house was blue. They had breakfast together every day, and then they each went home to work. In the evening, they met again for dinner.

Frida Kahlo was in an accident when she was younger, and she was often in great pain. Many of her paintings showed this. She died at the age of 47. Rivera was very disturbed by her death, and people said he aged suddenly. But the next year he married again. Two years later, Rivera died at the age of 71.

常起风暴。他们多次吵架、分居，甚至离了婚又复婚。报纸上常有"弗里达与迭戈"的花边新闻。他们住在墨西哥城，其住房是分开的，中间由一座桥连接起来。里韦拉的住房是粉红色的而卡洛的房子是蓝色的。他们每天一起共进早餐，然后各自回屋工作，晚上又到一起共进晚餐。

弗里达·卡洛年轻时出过一次事故，她经常得忍着剧痛作画，她的许多作品都表现出了这一点。卡洛47岁时去世。卡洛的死使里韦拉伤心不已，人们说他一下子变老了。但是，第二年他又结婚了。两年后，里韦拉去世，享年71岁。

---

stormy *adj.* 风暴的

separation *n.* 分居

37

Jim Thorpe

In 1950, Jim Thorpe was named the greatest American football player and the best athlete of the first half of the twentieth century. He was also an Olympic gold medal winner and a national hero. But Thorpe had many *tragedies* in his life. Even his greatest *achievements* did not make him rich or happy.

Jim Thorpe was a Native American. He was born in 1888 in an Indian Territory that is now Oklahoma. Like most Native American children then, he liked to fish, hunt, swim, and play games outdoors.

吉姆·索普

1950年吉姆·索普被命名为美国橄榄球的最佳球员和20世纪上半叶的最佳运动员。他还是奥林匹克运动会金牌得主和民族英雄。但他的一生是悲剧的一生,甚至他的巨大成功也未能给他带来财富和幸福。

吉姆·索普是土著美国人。1888年他出生在一块印第安人居留地上——位于现在的俄克拉荷马州。他和当时大多数美国土著人的孩子一样,喜欢打鱼、狩猎、游泳和户外运动。他非常健壮,但受到的正规教育十分有限。

tragedy *n.* 悲剧   achievement *n.* 成就

He was healthy and strong, but he had very little *formal* education.

Jim had a twin brother who died when he was nine years old. This was the first tragedy of his life, but not the last. By the time he was 16, his mother and father were also dead. Jim then went to a special school in Pennsylvania for Native American children. There, he learned to read and write and also began to play sports. Jim was poor, so he left school for two years to earn some money. During this time, he played on a baseball team. The team paid him only $15 a week. Soon he returned to

---

　　吉姆9岁时，他的孪生兄弟夭折了，这是他生活中的第一个却不是最后的悲剧。他16岁时，已是父母双亡。吉姆到了宾夕法尼亚州，在一所为土著美国儿童开设的特别学校上学，他在那里读书、写字并开始体育运动。吉姆很穷，为此他曾辍学两年去挣钱。这期间，他参加了棒球运动，棒球队每周只发给他15美元，不久他又回到学校接受教育。吉姆在许多运

---

formal *adj.* 正式的

school to complete his education. Jim was a star athlete in several sports, including baseball, running, wrestling, and football. He won many awards for his athletic ability, mainly for football. In many games, he scored all or most of the points for his team.

In 1912, when Jim Thorpe was 24 years old, he became part of the U.S. Olympic team. He competed in two very difficult events: the *pentathlon* and the *decathlon*. Both require great ability and strength. The pentathlon has five track and field events, including the long jump and the 1,500-meter race. The decathlon has ten track and field events, with running, jumping, and throwing contests.

动中都是体育明星，包括棒球、赛跑、摔跤和橄榄球。他有运动天赋，曾多次获奖，主要是在橄榄球方面。在许多比赛中，全部或绝大部分的分数都被他一人包揽。

1912年吉姆·索普24岁时，他成了美国奥林匹克运动队的一名成员。他参加两项铁人赛的竞赛：五项全能和十项全能。二者都需要极强的技能和体格。五项全能包括五项径赛和田赛，如跳远和1500米跑。十项全能包括十项径赛和田赛，如跑、跳和投掷运动等。

---

pentathlon *n.* 五项运动　　　　　　　　　decathlon *n.* 十项运动

People thought it was impossible for an athlete to compete in both the pentathlon and the decathlon. So everyone was surprised when Thorpe won gold medals in both events. When the King of Sweden presented Thorpe with his two gold medals, he said, "Sir, you are the greatest athlete in the world." Thorpe was a simple and honest man. He just answered, "Thanks, King."

When Thorpe came home he was an American hero. But all the *praise* did not last for very long. Less than a year later, there was another tragedy. A newspaper reporter found out that Thorpe had played baseball for money. People who earn money for playing sports are called professionals. At that time, professionals could not compete in the Olympics. Only *amateurs* were allowed. Officials decided that Thorpe had to return his gold medals. Many people

---

　　人们认为一个运动员既参加五项全能又参加十项全能运动竞赛是不可能的。因此，他在两项竞赛中都获得金牌时，大家都十分惊讶。瑞典国王给吉姆颁发两枚金牌时说道："先生，你是世界上最伟大的运动员。"吉姆是位朴实的人，他简短地回答道："谢谢，陛下。"

　　他回到家乡，一时成了美国英雄。但是，一切荣誉没有持续多久，不到一年，又一悲剧发生了。一报社记者报道说索普曾经为挣钱打棒球。通过参加运动挣钱的人叫作职业运动员。按规定，职业运动员不能参加奥林匹克竞赛，只有业余运动员才能获准参加。有关官员决定索普必须交回金牌。许多人认为这是不公平的。但是奥林匹克委员会仍然收缴了他的金牌并从成绩记录簿上抹去他的名字。

---

praise　*n.* 荣耀；赞扬　　　　　　　　　　　amateur　*n.* 业余爱好者

believed this was unfair. But the Olympic Committee took away his medals and removed his name from the record books.

Thorpe was devastated. At first he decided to stop playing sports. But he was an athlete and had few other skills, so he played *professional* baseball and football. Unfortunately, Thorpe had another great tragedy in his life. His three-year-old son died of the flu. Many people said that Thorpe never got over this loss.

Thorpe was an *outstanding* football player and helped to make football a popular sport in America. In 1929, he retired from football. He had several jobs and also gave speeches on sports and Native American issues. Thorpe was very proud of being a Native American. Unfortunately, some people did not treat him fairly because of his

---

索普精神崩溃了。起初他决定终止体育运动生涯。但他是个运动员，几乎没有其他技能。因此，他只好参加职业棒球和橄榄球运动。不幸的是，另一悲剧降临到他的头上，他三岁的儿子死于流感。人们说，吉姆一直没有摆脱掉这一巨大损失的阴影。

索普是个杰出的橄榄球队员，他还致力于推介橄榄球，使之成为美国人喜爱的一项运动。1929年，他从橄榄球运动中退役。他干过好几种工作，还做过关于体育运动和土著美国民族问题的演讲。索普为自己是一个本土的美国人而骄傲。遗憾的是，有些人因为种族问题对他不公平，这一点令他既伤心又愤怒。他永远忘不了奥林匹克委员会收回了他的金牌，他

---

professional *adj.* 职业的；专业的　　　　　　outstanding *adj.* 杰出的

race. This made him sad and angry. He also never forgot that the Olympic *Committee* took away his medals. He believed they had cheated him.

In 1951, Thorpe became sick with cancer. By that time, he had almost no money. Some groups who remembered his Olympic performance raised money to help him. Two years later, Thorpe died of a heart attack. He was 64 years old.

Many people tried to get Thorpe's medals back to him. But it never happened during his lifetime. Thirty years after his death, the medals were finally returned. Six of Thorpe's children attended the *ceremony*. His name was also put back in the 1912 Olympic record books.

认为他们欺骗了他。

1951年吉姆患了癌症。那时，他几乎身无分文。一些还记得他在奥林匹克运动中的出色表现的团体帮助他募集资金治病。两年后，索普死于心脏病，享年64岁。

许多人曾努力帮助索普要回金牌，他在世时却没有能实现。他去世30年后，金牌终于回归。他的6名子女参加了重授奖牌的仪式。他的名字又荣归1912年奥林匹克成绩记录簿上。

---

committee *n.* 委员会　　　　　　　　　　ceremony *n.* 典礼；仪式

38

Agatha Christie

Agatha Christie is often called the "Queen of *Crime*." But Christie was not a thief or a murderer. She was a very respectable woman. She earned this title because she wrote some of the most popular mysteries and *detective* stories in the world.

Agatha was born in 1890 in

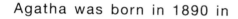

阿加莎·克里斯蒂

阿加莎·克里斯蒂常常被称为"犯罪王后"。不过，克里斯蒂并不是盗贼或凶手，她是一位非常受人尊敬的女性。她获此头衔是因为她撰写了一些世界上最受人欢迎的神秘侦探故事。

阿加莎1890年生于英国的德文郡。孩提时代，她就喜欢听故事和讲

crime *n.* 犯罪　　　　　　　　　　　　　detective *adj.* 侦探的

Devonshire, England. As a child, she loved to hear and tell stories. Agatha never went to school, but she was very bright. She loved books and taught herself to read before she was five years old.

Agatha wrote her first short story when she was 18 years old. Her first novel, *The Mysterious Affair at Styles*, was *published* in 1920. By then, she was married to Archibald Christie. Soon after, she wrote four more popular novels. In 1926, The Murder of Roger Ackroyd was published. Some people didn't like it because an unusual character was the *murderer*. Others called it one of the greatest detective stories of all time. It was the book that made her famous.

Christie was very successful. But her marriage was unhappy. Her husband, Archibald, was in love with a woman named Nancy Neele, and Agatha was devastated. She was also upset because

---

故事。阿加莎没有上过学，但她很聪明。她喜爱书籍，5岁之前就自学读书了。

阿加莎18岁时写了第一篇短篇故事。她的第一部小说《斯泰尔斯的神秘事件》于1920年出版。就在那时，她嫁给了阿奇博尔德·克里斯蒂。不久，她又写了4部畅销小说。1926年，《罗杰·艾克罗伊德谋杀案》出版了。有些人不喜欢这部小说，因为书中一位非同寻常的人物是凶手。另一些人则称这本书是空前的最佳侦探故事之一。而正是这本书使她声名鹊起。

克里斯蒂事业上如日中天，但她的婚姻却很不如意。她丈夫阿奇博

---

publish *v.* 出版   murderer *n.* 凶手

some people didn't like her new book. On December 3, 1926, Agatha Christie did something very mysterious. She got into her car, drove away, and *disappeared*. Someone found her car the next day. Christie's coat was on the seat and the car lights were on. For ten days, thousands of police officers and *volunteers* looked for her. The newspapers wrote stories about the real-life mystery of the mystery writer.

On the eleventh day, someone found Christie at a hotel. She was talking with other guests and acting very normal. She said her name was Teresa Neele, the same last name as her husband's lover! Christie never explained her actions, but she and her husband got divorced a short time later. In 1930, she married Max Mallowan. He

---

尔德爱上了一位叫南希·尼尔的女人，阿加莎受到了沉重的打击。她还深感不悦的是，一些人不喜欢她的新书。1926年12月3日，阿加莎·克里斯蒂做出了一件很神秘的事。她钻进自己的汽车并开走，继而失踪了。第二天，有人发现了她的汽车，克里斯蒂的外套放在车座上，车灯仍然亮着。数千名警察和志愿者寻找她达十天之久，各家报纸纷纷报道对这位侦探作家所展开的真情实景的侦探。

　　在第十一天，有人在一家旅馆里发现了克里斯蒂，她正在和其他客人聊天，而且谈吐正常。她说她叫特里萨·尼尔，竟然和她丈夫的情人同姓！克里斯蒂一直没有解释她为什么这么做，但不久，她便和丈夫离婚

---

disappear *v.* 失踪

volunteer *n.* 志愿者

was an *archeologist*, a scientist who studies ancient cultures. He was 14 years younger than she was. They were very happy together. Christie once said, "It's wonderful to be married to an archeologist— the older you get, the more interested he is in you."

Christie tried to write a novel for Christmas each year. She wrote for over 50 years and produced a *remarkable* amount of work. She wrote 66 novels, 15 plays, and 157 short stories. Once, one of Christie's books saved someone's life. A little girl was very sick. The doctors tried everything, but she only got worse. One of the girl's nurses was reading Christie's mystery story *The Pale Horse*. In the story, the murderer kills his victim with a poison called thallium. The victim's symptoms described in the book were like the little

---

了。1930年，她与马克斯·马洛温结婚了。马克斯是考古学家，即一位研究古代文化的科学家，小她14岁。他们在一起很快活。克里斯蒂曾经说过："嫁给一位考古学家简直妙极了——你越老，他对你越感兴趣。"

克里斯蒂倾力为每年的圣诞节写一本小说。她创作了五十多年，奉献出数量可观的一批作品。她写了66部小说、15部戏剧和157篇短篇故事。一次，克里斯蒂的书还救了一个人的生命。一个小姑娘病得很厉害，医生们尽管绞尽了脑汁，但每况愈下。病人的一位女护士那时正在读克里斯蒂的《白马酒店》。故事中，凶手用一种叫铊的毒药残杀其受害者。书中对

---

archeologist *n.* 考古学家　　　　　　　　　　remarkable *adj.* 杰出的

girl's symptoms. The nurse thought, "Did this little girl *swallow* thallium?"She told the doctors about the case. They tried a new medicine and saved the girl's life.

Agatha Christie liked to write stories about two detectives. Their names were Miss Marple and Hercule Poirot. Miss Marple is a quiet, unmarried woman who lives in a small village. She notices everything that happens. She is very bright and always solves the crimes before the police do. Hercule Poirot is a retired Belgian detective. He has a very good opinion of himself and is very neat and meticulous. Readers loved the *characters* of Miss Marple and Hercule Poirot and always wanted to read their next cases.

受害者症状的描写很像小姑娘的症状。那位护士想："是不是小姑娘吞食了铊?"她把这个情况报告给医生,他们试用了新药,果然挽救了小姑娘的命。

阿加莎·克里斯蒂喜欢写两位名探的故事,他们的名字是马普尔小姐和大侦探波洛。马普尔小姐是一位文静的未婚女子,住在一个小村庄里。她留意案件发生时的每一细节,聪明过人的她总是先于警察破案。大侦探波洛则是一位退休的比利时侦探。他很自傲,但非常有头脑,破案条理清楚而巧妙,谨慎而周密。读者们都很喜爱马普尔小姐和大侦探波洛这样的人物,总是渴望阅读他们的下一个破案故事。

---

swallow *v.* 吞下

character *n.* 人物;角色

Sometime in the 1940s, Christie wrote the last cases for Miss Marple and Hercule Poirot. Readers wanted more of these stories, so Christie asked for the books to be published after she died. She died on January 12, 1976. Both books became *immediate* best sellers.

Agatha Christie's books have sold over a billion *copies* in English and another billion in over 45 other languages. Her books still continue to sell. She is now the most popular British author in the world and the fifth best selling author of all time. That is why some call her the "Queen of Crime."

在20世纪40年代的一段时间里，克里斯蒂写了马普尔小姐和大侦探波洛的最后一批案件。读者们还想读更多的这类故事，因此，克里斯蒂要求在她死后出版这些书。她于1976年1月12日逝世。这两本书立即成为畅销书。

阿加莎·克里斯蒂著作的英文版图书已销售十亿多册，其他四十五种文字的多种译本也销售了十亿册，她的作品的销售量仍然历久不衰。她是当今世界上最受欢迎的英国作家之一，在有史以来的畅销书作家排行榜上名列第五。这就是人们称她"犯罪王后"的缘由。

---

immediate *adj.* 立即的   copy *n.* 一册；副本

39

Louis Armstrong

Louis Armstrong was one of the greatest jazz *trumpet* players in the world. He traveled to many countries and helped to make jazz popular everywhere. Louis was born in 1901 in New Orleans, Louisiana. His family was poor, and his father left when Louis was very young. Louis sang on street corners and worked at small jobs to earn money.

Life got even harder for Louis. On New Year's Eve, 1913, he fired a gun into the air. He did it for fun and nobody was hurt. But the police *arrested* him and put him in a home for problem children.

路易斯·阿姆斯特朗

 易斯·阿姆斯特朗是世界上最著名的爵士乐小号演奏家之一。他周游许多国家，大力促进爵士音乐在全球各地的流行。路易斯于1901年出生在路易斯安那州的新奥尔良。路易斯家境贫苦，很小的时候他的父亲就离家出走了。为了挣点钱，路易斯在街头卖唱，并干些零活儿。

对路易斯来说，生活更加艰难。在1913年的新年除夕，他向空中放了一枪。他放枪只是为了好玩，也没有伤着谁。但是，警察把他抓起来，

---

trumpet *n.* 小号；喇叭   arrest *v.* 逮捕

This event changed Louis's life forever. At the home, Louis learned to play the *cornet*, a musical instrument that is like a trumpet. When he left there 18 months later, he started to play in small jazz bands. Louis Armstrong was so good that

the great cornet player Joe "king" Oliver noticed him. Oliver gave Armstrong lessons and helped him learn about the music business.

By age 18, Armstrong quit his other jobs and started to play the cornet full time. In 1922, "King" Oliver asked Armstrong to join him in Chicago. It was a great *opportunity* for Armstrong. Soon Louis

---

关进了失足少年教化所。这件事永久地改变了路易斯的生活。在教化所里，路易斯学会了吹短号—— 一种类似小号的乐器。18个月后，他离开了那里，开始到一些小的爵士乐队演奏。路易斯·阿姆斯特朗演奏得非常出色，连著名的短号演奏家、外号叫"国王"的乔·奥利佛都注意到他了。奥利佛给阿姆斯特朗授课，帮助他学会音乐经纪。

　　阿姆斯特朗18岁时辞去了别的工作，开始专职演奏短号。1922年，"国王"奥利佛邀请阿姆斯特朗加盟他在芝加哥的乐队。对于阿姆斯特朗

---

cornet *n.* （乐器）短号　　　　　　　　opportunity *n.* 时机；机会

Armstrong was more popular than "King" Oliver. For the next few years, Armstrong worked in Chicago, New Orleans, and New York. He played with the most popular musicians of his time. He learned a lot about music. He also began to play the trumpet.

In 1925, Armstrong started his own band called the Hot Five. The band was very successful, and Armstrong became world famous. When he returned to New York in 1929, he was a jazz *idol*.

Armstrong worked very hard in New York. Every evening he was the star in the musical Hot Chocolate. After the show, he went to work at a famous *nightclub*. Soon he was traveling all around the country. He also performed in many Hollywood movies. He often slept too little and ate and drank too much. But he was still strong even when he got older. Armstrong was always aware of his health.

来说，这是一个千载难逢的机遇。很快，路易斯·阿姆斯特朗的风头甚至更盛于"国王"奥利佛了。在随后的几年里，阿姆斯特朗在芝加哥、新奥尔良和纽约演奏。他与当时最受欢迎的音乐大师们同台表演，学到许多音乐方面的知识。同时，他开始演奏小号。

1925年，阿姆斯特朗成立了自己的乐队，起名为"当红五人组合"。乐队大获成功，阿姆斯特朗因而闻名世界。1929年回到纽约时，他已成了爵士乐的偶像人物。

阿姆斯特朗在纽约干得很卖劲儿。每天晚上，他都是"劲歌巧克力"音乐节目的明星。演出之后，他又到一家著名夜总会演奏。不久，他演遍全国。他还在许多好莱坞的电影中饰演角色。他常常睡眠不足，却暴饮暴食。但他年纪大时，身体仍然很结实。阿姆斯特朗一向注意自己的健康，他害怕

---

idol *n.* 偶像   nightclub *n.* 夜总会

He was afraid of *germs* and always carried the mouthpiece of his trumpet in a clean handkerchief in his pocket.

People everywhere loved Armstrong. They loved his warm-hearted personality and his happy smile. They also loved his big, wide mouth. People started to call him "satchelmouth" because his mouth was as big as a large *satchel* or bag. Then they shortened it to "Satchmo."

Armstrong also became famous for his rough singing voice. He sang more as he got older, because it was harder for him to play the trumpet. He also created a new kind of singing called "scat." In scat, a singer sings nonsense syllables instead of words ("ba doo ba dooo ba"). One story says that Armstrong invented it by mistake. One day he dropped his music while he was recording a song. He started to sing nonsense syllables, and scat was born.

病菌，总是把自己的号嘴儿包在一块干净的手绢中揣在口袋里。

各地的人都喜欢阿姆斯特朗。他们喜欢他的热心肠性格和快乐的微笑，也喜欢他那又大又宽的嘴。人们开始叫他"布袋嘴"，因为他的嘴巴看起来像书包或口袋那么大。后来，这个词的发音被简化为"沙契牟"。

阿姆斯特朗也以他的粗犷歌喉而闻名。他年岁大时唱得更多，因为吹小号对他来说日渐艰难了。他还创造了一种新式的唱法，叫作"斯卡特"(scat)。在"斯卡特"唱法中，歌手不唱歌词，而唱些无实际语义的音节(如"ba doo ba dooo ba"，声如"吧嘟吧嘟吧")。有人说，阿姆斯特朗是因为将错就错才发明了这种唱法的。一天，当他正在录制一首歌曲时，他忘记词儿了，便唱出无语义的音节，于是，"斯卡特"便诞生了。

---

germ *n.* 细菌　　　　　　　　　　　satchel *n.* 书包；小背包

People around the world wanted to hear Louis Armstrong. He played for England's King George VI. He toured the Middle East, Asia, and South America. On his world tour in the 1950s, people called him "America's *Ambassador* of Goodwill." In his 1960 African tour, 100,000 people heard him play in Ghana. But fame and money didn't change Armstrong. He always came back to his *modest* home in a run-down neighborhood in New York City. He said he wanted "to be with my people."

After a career of more than 50 years, Louis died in New York City in 1971. He made over 2,000 recordings and more than 30 movies. People everywhere *mourned* his death. In New Orleans, he received a traditional jazz musician's funeral with jazz bands playing and people dancing in the street.

全世界的人都希望欣赏到路易斯·阿姆斯特朗的演奏。他为英国国王乔治六世表演过。他去过中东、亚洲和南美作巡回演出。在20世纪50年代，他到世界各地巡回演出时，人们赞誉他为"美国友好大使"。1960年他在非洲巡回演出时，在加纳有十万人听他演奏。但是，名誉和金钱并没有改变阿姆斯特朗，他经常回到位于纽约的那一片年久失修的街区和朴实无华的家中。他说，他图的是"要和自己家人待在一起"。

经历了五十多年的演奏生涯之后，路易斯于1971年在纽约市辞世。他灌制过两千多张唱片，拍摄过三十多部电影。各地的人们都在悼念他的逝世。在新奥尔良，他得到了传统爵士乐师葬礼的厚遇，爵士乐乐队为他演奏，人们在街上用舞步为他送葬。

---

ambassador *n.* 大使　　　　modest *adj.* 朴素的；朴实的
mourn *v.* 哀悼

Umm Kulthum

People called Umm Kulthum "the voice of Egypt." She was born in 1904 in a small village in Egypt. She came from a poor family. Her father was the imam, or *prayer* leader at the local *mosque*. To earn extra money, he sang religious songs for

---

乌姆·库勒苏姆

人们称乌姆·库勒苏姆为"埃及之声"。1904年她出生在埃及的一个小村庄里，家境贫寒。她父亲是"伊玛目"，即当地清真寺领头做礼拜的人。为了多挣点钱，他还为婚礼和其他庆典唱颂宗教歌曲。

---

prayer *n.* 祈祷

mosque *n.* 清真寺

weddings and other celebrations.

Umm's father taught his son to sing, so they could sing together at the celebrations. Umm listened to them and soon learned the songs by heart. One day her father heard her singing. He decided to teach Umm too. Once when her brother got sick, Umm sang in his place. Her voice was *exceptionally* strong and clear. Everybody listened in silence. They thought her voice was a gift from God. Soon Umm became the star singer. But no one knew that Umm was a girl. She dressed as a boy because her father thought it was wrong for a girl to sing in public.

Umm and her father began to earn a lot of money. They traveled to other villages so Umm could *perform*. People said that they should go to Cairo because Cairo was the center for the music business. At

---

　　乌姆的父亲教他的儿子唱歌，以便他们能一起在庆典上唱歌。乌姆听着他们唱歌，很快，她就能把那些歌都背下来了。一天，她父亲听到她在唱歌，就决定也教乌姆。有时她兄弟病了，乌姆就顶替他唱。她的歌喉特别清脆嘹亮，每个人都安静地聆听。大家认为，她的嗓音是神灵赋予她的。乌姆很快就成了歌星，但是，谁也不知道乌姆是个女孩。她打扮成一个男孩，因为她父亲认为，女孩在公众面前唱歌是不对的。

　　乌姆和父亲开始挣大钱了。他们巡回到别的村庄，以便让乌姆表演。

---

exceptionally *adv.* 特殊地　　　　　　　　　　　perform *v.* 表演

first, the family did not want to go because they knew no one in the big city. Finally, in 1923, they decided to move.

In the beginning, Umm Kulthum sang the religious songs she learned from her father. But people said that this kind of music was old-fashioned. So she decided to compete with the other famous singers of the time. She hired teachers, took lessons, and practiced. Then she started to sing modern love songs. She also dressed in elegant clothes and held a long silk handkerchief. This handkerchief became her *trademark*. Kulthum's career really started when she began to make records. By 1928, she was the most popular professional singer in Cairo.

By 1934, radio and movies began to come to Cairo. Kulthum was popular in both. She *broadcast* a live concert on the first Thursday of

---

人们说，他们应该到开罗去，因为开罗是音乐界的中心。起初，全家都不愿意去，因为他们在那个大城市里谁都不认识。终于在1923年，他们决定搬家了。

一开始，乌姆·库勒苏姆演唱从父亲那里学来的宗教歌曲。但人们说，这种音乐太守旧了，所以，她决定与当时其他的著名歌手竞争。她聘了几位老师，上音乐课并勤奋练习。然后，她开始唱现代的爱情歌曲。她还穿着典雅的服装，手中拿着一条长长的丝绸手绢。这块手绢遂成了她的商标和象征。库勒苏姆的事业真正开始于她录制唱片之时。到1928年，她成了开罗最受欢迎的职业歌手。

到1934年，在开罗开始出现广播和电影，库勒苏姆在这两类表演中

---

trademark n. 商标   broadcast v. 播放；播送

every month. People called it "Umm Kulthum Night." When she sang on the radio, people said that life in the Arab world came to a stop. In 1935, she began to work on the first of six films.

Kulthum chose her songs carefully. Some were popular songs, others were from *classical* Arab pieces. Her songs connected the people of her country to their history. That is why they called her "the voice of Egypt." Kulthum always sang from her heart. She did not even let her musicians learn to read music because she wanted the music to come from their hearts.

People always wanted to know about Kulthum's personal life. But her *privacy* was important to her. Once one of the king's uncles proposed marriage to her. However, the royal family did not agree to the marriage, and she was deeply hurt. Soon after, she married one

---

都很受欢迎。每个月的第一个星期四，她都播出一个实况音乐会，人们称它为"乌姆·库勒苏姆之夜"。人们都说，当她在广播里唱歌时，整个阿拉伯世界的生活都戛然而止。1935年，她开始为其6部电影中的第一部工作。

库勒苏姆仔细地选择歌曲。有些是流行歌曲，有些则是古典阿拉伯歌曲。她的歌曲将埃及人民与他们的历史连接在一起，这就是为什么人们管她叫"埃及之声"的原因。库勒苏姆总是从内心唱出歌声，她甚至不让她的乐师们对着乐谱演出，因为她想让音乐从他们的心灵深处发出。

人们总想了解库勒苏姆的个人生活，但她的隐私对于她是至关重要的。一次，国王的一个叔叔想向她求婚，然而，王族却不同意这桩婚事，这事深深地伤了库勒苏姆的心。不久之后，她嫁给了她的一位乐师，但这

---

classical *adj.* 古典的　　　　　　　　privacy *n.* 隐私

of her musicians, but the marriage only lasted a few days. Finally, in 1954, she married Hasan al-Hifnawi, who was one of her doctors. This marriage was successful.

Kulthum had several health problems, but she continued to sing into her seventies. Her concerts always started late in the evening and lasted from three to six hours. During her last concert in December 1972, she felt faint but finished the concert anyway. Kulthum planned to sing again but never did. She died in 1975. Four million people filled the streets of Cairo at her *funeral*. More people came to her funeral than to the funeral of President Nasser! Even today millions of people in the Arab world listen to the songs of Umm Kulthum.

桩婚姻只持续了几天。最终，在1954年，她嫁给了哈桑·希夫纳维——她的一名医生。这桩婚姻很成功。

库勒苏姆身患多种疾病，但她一直唱到七十多岁。她的音乐会总是在晚上很迟才开场，一般持续三到六个小时。在1972年12月的最后一场音乐会上，她感到晕眩，但还是坚持到音乐会结束。库勒苏姆曾打算再次登台演唱，但再也没有可能了。她于1975年去世，参加葬礼的四百万人挤满了开罗的大街小巷，比参加纳赛尔总统葬礼的人还要多！甚至到今天，阿拉伯的千百万人仍在欣赏乌姆·库勒苏姆的歌曲。

---

funeral *n.* 葬礼

41

Howard Hughes

People say that money cannot buy happiness. This was true for Howard Hughes. He was one of the richest and most powerful men of his time. He had everything: good looks, *charm*, success, power, and a lot of money. But he didn't have love or friendship because he couldn't buy them. All his life he used his money to *control* everything and everyone around him. In the end, he lost

霍华德·休斯

人们说，金钱买不来幸福。对于霍华德·休斯来说，确实如此。他是他那代人中最富有、权势最大的人物之一。他应有尽有：相貌英俊，魅力超群，一帆风顺，有权有势，富甲天下。但是他没有爱情和友谊，因为他用金钱买不到。他一辈子用钱财控制周围的一切和每一个人。最终，他对一切甚至对自己都失去了控制。

charm *n.* 魅力

control *v.* 控制

control of everything, even himself.

Howard Hughes was born in 1905 in Houston, Texas. His father started the Hughes Tool Company. He was a workaholic and made a lot of money. He bought everything he wanted. He even gave money to schools so Howard could get into them. From his father, Howard learned to be a successful but ruthless businessman. Hughes's mother, Allene, also had a big influence on his life. Howard was her only child. She protected him and gave him everything. Unfortunately, Allene had mental problems. She was afraid of germs and disease. She was *obsessed* with Howard's health, and he became obsessed with it too.

Allene died when Howard was 16 years old. Two years later his father died. Hughes *inherited* Hughes Tool Company. Then he married Ella Rice. He and Ella moved to Los Angeles, California. It was there that Howard Hughes began to become a legend.

　　霍华德·休斯于1905年出生在德克萨斯州的休斯敦。他父亲开办了休斯工具公司，他是一个工作狂，挣了许多钱，可以说是想要买什么就买什么。他甚至把钱送给几所学校好让霍华德能入学。霍华德从父亲那里学到的是成为一名成功却冷酷无情的商人的本事。霍华德的母亲艾伦娜也对他的生活产生了巨大的影响。霍华德是她唯一的孩子，她呵护着霍华德，要什么给什么。不幸的是，艾伦娜有精神病。她向来对细菌和疾病有着恐惧感，总是担心霍华德的健康，以致霍华德也总是担心自己的健康。

　　霍华德16岁时，艾伦娜去世了。两年后，他的父亲也故去。霍华德继承了休斯工具公司。之后，他娶了埃拉·里斯为妻。他和埃拉搬到加利福尼亚州的洛杉矶，正是在那里，霍华德·休斯开始成为一名传奇人物。

---

obsess　*v.* 使（某人）牵挂、惦念、着迷或困扰　　　　　　inherit　*v.* 继承

Hughes began to *invest* his money in movies. He became an important producer soon after he moved to California. He worked hard, but he also played hard. He became obsessed with power and control. When he couldn't get something legally, he gave money to politicians and businessmen so they would help him. He owned a lot of businesses, including airplane companies, a movie studio, Las Vegas hotels, gold and silver mines, and radio and television stations. Once he bought a television studio so he could watch movies all night. He also bought a hotel because he wanted to stay in his favorite room for one weekend.

Hughes loved the wild Hollywood life and *dated* many famous movie stars. Of course, his marriage ended very quickly. He asked every woman to marry him on the first date. Hughes used people for his pleasure and didn't treat them very well, so he had no real friends.

　　休斯开始投资电影业。他搬到加州不久，就成了一位重要的制片人。他工作很努力，娱乐也求尽兴。休斯逐渐迷恋于权力和控制，当他不能通过合法渠道达到目的时，他便贿赂政要和商人，以便让他们帮忙。他拥有许多企业，包括几家航空公司、一座电影制片厂、拉斯维加斯的酒店、金矿银矿以及电台和电视台。他曾经买下一个电视演播室，为的是能整夜地看电影。他还买下了一家酒店，仅因为他想在他最喜欢的房间里度过一个周末。

　　休斯喜欢狂野的好莱坞生活以及与许多著名影星幽会。当然，他的婚姻只是昙花一现，他与每个女人第一次幽会就要求对方嫁给他。休斯把人们视为他寻欢作乐的工具，从不善待他们，所以，他没有真正的朋友。

---

invest *v.* 投资   date *v.* 和……约会

Howard Hughes loved fast cars and airplanes. He was a *daredevil* pilot and risked his life many times. He set many flying records, including the fastest flight around the world at the time. Reporters loved to write about the rich, handsome playboy pilot. But Hughes's love of adventure also hurt him. He was in many airplane and car crashes—14 in all. Once he almost died when his plane crashed into a house. Hughes had serious physical and mental problems because of these accidents.

When Hughes couldn't control a situation, he became ill. He had a lot of mental problems. Once in a while, he just ran away. Sometimes he was gone for months. He changed his name and worked at simple jobs for a while. Then he returned home.

Hughes was very *eccentric*. Every day he got worse and worse. He had the same dinner every night: a steak, a baked potato, and

---

霍华德·休斯喜欢开高速车和飞机。他是一位胆大如天的飞行员并且多次蛮勇地去冒险，他创造了许多飞行记录，包括当时最快的环球飞行。记者们都喜欢报道这位富有的、英俊的花花公子飞行员。但是，休斯的冒险嗜好也伤害了他自己。他经历了多次车祸和坠机——总共14次。有一次，他的飞机撞上一所房子，几乎丧命。由于这些事故，休斯在身体上和精神上都遗留下严重的问题。

当休斯不能控制局势时，他就会生病。他有许多精神上的障碍，他不时地离家出走，有时一走就是几个月。他会埋名隐姓，外出去做一段时间的零工，然后再回到家中。

休斯行为怪异，而且病态每况愈下。每晚他都吃同样的饭菜：一块牛排，一个烤马铃薯，以及12粒豌豆。他要求什么东西都必须是完美无

---

daredevil *adj.* 胆大妄为的；蛮干的　　　　eccentric *adj.* 古怪的

12 peas. Everything always had to be perfect. His tomatoes had to be cut exactly one-quarter inch thick. His sandwiches had to be cut into exact triangles. As Hughes got older, his behavior became even more strange. Once he stayed in the same room for two and a half years. He was afraid of germs too. He hired people just to kill flies. He also covered everything with tissues. Then he wore the empty tissue boxes on his feet! Sometimes he refused to wear clothes or cut his fingernails and hair.

Howard Hughes died on an airplane in 1976. He was on the way to see a doctor. He was very sick from living such a strange life. Sadly, the rich, handsome playboy lost his mind, his health, and his *dignity*. He loved no one and no one loved him. Howard Hughes had bought everything in his life, except happiness.

缺的。他吃西红柿必须切得正好是1/4英寸厚，三明治必须切成等边三角形。随着年岁越来越大，休斯变得更加古怪。有一次，他竟然在同一个房间里一待就是两年半；他对细菌也有恐慌症；他雇了一些人专门负责打苍蝇；所有物品他都用纸巾去盖上，然后，他把空纸巾盒穿在脚上！有时，他拒绝穿衣服、剪指甲和理发。

霍华德·休斯于1976年在一架飞机上逝世，当时正是在去看医生的途中。由于过着这种奇怪的日子，他已病入膏肓。可悲的是，这位富有的、漂亮的花花公子失去了理智，失去了健康，也失去了尊严。他其实谁也不爱，也没有人爱他。在他的一生中，霍华德·休斯什么都买到了，就是没有买到幸福。

---

dignity   *n.* 尊严

Soichiro Honda

Soichiro Honda was born in 1906 in a small village in Japan. It was so small that it didn't even have *electricity*. His family was poor. Soichiro had eight brothers and sisters. Sadly, five of them died when they were young because they did not have good *medical* care. When

本田宗一郎

本田宗一郎1906年出生于日本的一个小村庄。村庄很小，连电都没有。他家很穷，宗一郎一共有8个兄弟姐妹，不幸的是，由于缺医少药，他们中的5个夭折了。宗一郎8岁时，平生第一次见到汽车，他感到非常惊讶。在随后的50年中，他一直都喜欢这种靠轮子行驶的机械。

---

electricity　*n.* 电；电学　　　　　　　medical　*adj.* 医学的；药的

Soichiro was eight years old, he saw his first automobile. He was amazed by it. For the next 50 years, he loved machines on wheels.

When he was 15 years old, Soichiro left his village to work at an auto repair shop in Tokyo. It was then that Honda discovered motorcycles. He spent all of his free time fixing and riding motorcycles. He returned to his village six years later to open his own garage. Soon he owned several shops and had over 50 *employees*.

At the same time, he began to build and race motorcycles and cars. Honda loved to race, and he became one of Japan's most competitive drivers. In 1936, his race car crashed while he was driving 100 miles per hour. Half of Honda's face was crushed, and he had other serious injuries. It took him a year and a half to *recover*.

15岁的时候，宗一郎离开家乡到东京一家汽车修理铺干活。正是在这个时候，本田涉足了摩托车行业，他的所有业余时间都花费在装修和驾驶摩托车上。6年以后，他回到家乡，开办了自己的修理部。不久，他就拥有了几家店铺，雇了五十多人。

与此同时，他开始制造摩托车和汽车，还举行赛会。本田喜欢比赛，并且成为日本最佳的参赛车手之一。1936年，他的汽车撞毁了，当时他正在以每小时100英里的速度驾驶。本田的半边脸都撞破了，还有其他几处重伤，过了一年半他才康复。出事以后，他的家人乞求他放弃比赛。他

---

employee *n.* 雇员　　　　　　　recover *v.* 恢复

After this, his family begged him to give up racing. He looked for a less dangerous job and finally decided to become a manufacturer.

At first, he manufactured engine parts. The Japanese navy used a lot of his engine parts in World War II. In 1948, after the war, he started the Honda Motor Company. He started the company with only $3,300. He made his first machines from engine parts that the military did not need after the war. These machines were not real motorcycles; they were bicycles with motors. People bought them because they needed a *reliable* form of transportation.

As Honda's business grew, he began to make different types of motorcycles. By 1950, his motorcycles were selling all over Japan. But there were 50 other motorcycle makers in Japan at the time. In 1958, Honda designed a *lightweight* motorcycle called the Super Cub.

找了一份不太危险的工作，并且最终决定当制造商。

刚开始，他是以制造发动机部件起家的。在第二次世界大战中，日本海军使用了他的许多发动机部件。战后，在1948年，他开创了本田摩托公司，公司当时的启动资金只有3 300美元。他使用军方战后不再使用的发动机部件制造了第一批车。当时这批车还不是真正的摩托车，只算是带马达的自行车，人们因需要一种可以依赖的交通工具而买这些车。

随着本田的生意做得越来越大，他便开始制造不同型号的摩托车。到1950年，他的摩托车销售遍及日本全国。但是，日本当时还有另外的50家摩托车生产厂。1958年，本田设计了一种轻便型摩托车，起名为"超强小兽"。这是一次巨大的成功，本田也因而赚了许多钱。两年后，本田

---

reliable *adj.* 可靠的；可信赖的　　　　　　　　lightweight *adj.* 轻量的

It was a huge success and Honda made a lot of money. Two years later, Honda built the world's biggest motorcycle factory in Japan.

By the 1960s, the Super Cub was popular all over Asia. But Honda wanted the motorcycle to be popular all over the world. In Europe, he put his motorcycles in difficult races to show how good they were. In the United States, he tried a different method. He used a magazine *ad* with the words "You Meet the Nicest People on a Honda." It showed ordinary Americans such as students, businessmen, and older people all riding happily on the Honda Super Cub. The ad appeared in many popular magazines.

Readers who had never ridden a motorcycle saw the ad. The ad showed that motorcycles were not just for crazy young people who wore black *leather* jackets. They were good for other people too. The company sold thousands of motorcycles to new riders. Honda then

---

在日本建起了世界上最大的摩托车制造厂。

到了20世纪60年代，超强小兽风靡整个亚洲，但是，本田想让他的摩托车流行全世界。在欧洲，他将他的摩托车投入到最艰难的比赛中去，以表明这些车的性能有多么好。在美国，他则采取了另一种办法。他采用杂志广告，广告词是"骑本田摩托，访至爱亲朋"。广告上展示出美国的老百姓风采，像学生、商人和老年人等都高兴地骑着本田超强小兽。这份广告登载在许多流行杂志上。

从来没有骑过摩托车的读者们都看得到这个广告，该广告表达的创意是：摩托车不仅仅是身穿黑皮来克的狂放青年的坐骑，其他人也可以享用。公司向新客户卖出了几千辆摩托车。本田随后又将广告在电视上播

---

ad (advertisement) 广告

leather *n.* 皮革

started to put the ads on television. This was also very successful. For example, he put an ad for his motorcycle on during the Academy Awards program. Millions of people watched that program, and on the next day, sales of the motorcycle went up *tremendously*. By 1968, Honda had sold 1 million motorcycles in the United States.

In 1963, his company started to make cars. In 1972, it produced the Civic; the next year, the Accord; and then in 1978, the Prelude. Soon, the company was one of the world's biggest automobile makers. Honda was also famous for his business style. He believed that workers and bosses should have a close relationship. He also thought it was important to encourage workers to do their best.

In 1973, Soichiro Honda retired as president of his company. He died in 1991. Honda was very important to Japan's recent history. He and many other business leaders helped make Japan into a leading industrial nation.

出，再次大获成功。例如，在奥斯卡奖颁奖电视节目中，他插入了摩托车广告。数以百万计的人观看了这个节目，第二天，摩托车的销售量便急剧攀升。到了1968年，本田在美国共销售了100万辆摩托车。

1963年，他的公司开始生产小汽车。1972年，"思域"(CMc)诞生了；第二年，"雅阁"(Accord)也问世了；接下来在1978年，"先驱"(Prelude)也被推出。不久后，公司就成为世界上最大的汽车制造厂家之一，本田也以其经营理念而闻名遐迩。他认为，工人和老板应该保持一种密切关系；他还认为，调动工人的最大积极性是很重要的。

1973年，本田宗一郎从公司董事长的职位上退了下来。他于1991年逝世。本田在日本的近代发展史上起了重要的作用，他和许多其他商业巨头促使日本成为先进的工业大国。

---

tremendously *adv.* 非常；惊人地